THE ALAN TURING
CODEBREAKER'S
PUZZLE BOOK

This edition published in 2017 by Arcturus Publishing Limited
26/27 Bickels Yard, 151–153 Bermondsey Street,
London SE1 3HA

Copyright © Arcturus Holdings Limited
Compiled by Any Puzzle Media Ltd

AD005831UK

Printed in the UK

Contents

Foreword

Alan Turing's last published paper was about puzzles. It was written for the popular science magazine Penguin Science News, and its theme is to explain to the general reader that while many mathematical problems will be solvable, it is not possible ahead of time to know whether any particular problem will be solvable or not. He illustrates his point using various homely things such as a tangled knot of string, and the sliding-squares puzzle where you have to restore the pattern by moving squares into an empty space. So, and with neat symmetry, Alan Turing's last paper covers the same subject as his first, in which – as well as dealing with provability testing for mathematical theorems – he set out what is now regarded as a blueprint for a programmable computer.

Alan Turing's role in the development of computers in the mid-twentieth century is well known, as is his work at Bletchley Park in unravelling one of the most strategically important puzzles of World War II, the Enigma cipher machine. The Enigma machine used a different cipher for every letter in a message; the only way to decipher a message was to know how the machine had been set up at the start of encryption, and then to follow the mechanical process of the machine. The codebreakers had to find this out, and the answer was not in the back of the book. Although they did not have computers to help them, with Alan Turing's help new electrical and electronic devices were invented which sifted out impossible and unlikely combinations and so reduced the puzzle to a manageable size. And the experience with these new machines laid the foundation for the development of electronic digital computers in the post-war years.

Computers are now commonplace, not only in the workplace and on a desk at home, in a smartphone or tablet, but in almost every piece of modern machinery. Teaching people computer skills and coding are now considered obvious elements of the curriculum. Except that this is not so, in all parts of the world. In Africa, access to computers in schools is extremely variable, and in some countries there is little or no opportunity for students to have hands-on experience of a real computer. For example, in 2007 in Kenya, 11% of schools had computers; in Malawi, it was only 2%.

The Turing Trust, a charity founded by Alan Turing's great-nephew James in 2009, aims to confront these challenges in a practical way which pays homage to Alan Turing's legacy in computer development. The Turing Trust provides still-working, used computers to African schools, enabling computer labs to be built in rural areas where students would otherwise be taught about computers with blackboard and chalk. The computers are refurbished and provided with an e-library of resources relevant to the local curriculum, and then sent out to give a new purpose and bring opportunity to underprivileged communities.

Thank you for buying this book and supporting the Turing Trust.

Sir Dermot Turing

August 2017

To find out more, visit *www.turingtrust.co.uk*

Introduction

ABOUT THE PUZZLES

The puzzles in this book are different from those you will typically come across elsewhere. Instead of being told exactly what to do, here part of the challenge is to work out the rules of each puzzle for yourself. That doesn't mean you have to guess, but rather you need to tease out how to solve each one from the hints that are hidden on the page.

Every puzzle in this book has both a number and a title. The number is simply for cross-referencing with the hints and solutions, but the title can be important – incredibly important, in some cases, where it may be the only hint you get as to what to do.

The puzzles are extremely varied, but there are inevitably some repeated mechanics, such as anagrams, or inserted or deleted letters. As you work your way through the book you should find your puzzle-solving skills gradually improving.

PUZZLE DIFFICULTY

There are five chapters of puzzles, and – as hinted at by the chapter titles – they become progressively more difficult. Depending on your experience you may be able to dive right into the final chapter, but if you fancy a gentler introduction then it's probably best to start with the first chapter, at least until you get into the flow of it.

With the exception of a series of puzzles in chapter 4, all of which are clearly marked, it doesn't matter what order you solve the puzzles in – so you can jump around as you please. If you don't see how to get started on a puzzle, why not leave it for another time and try the next one instead?

HINTS

When you get stuck – and you will definitely get stuck at some point – there are three things you can do. First, you can take a break, or chat it over with someone else who might have a fresh point of view or idea. Second, you can take a look at the solutions – which work on a step-by-step basis, so reading just a bit of a solution can be a fair method to get you started for some puzzles, without giving the entire game away. Or third, you can turn to the special hints section, in the middle of the book.

Each hint is broken down into a number of bulleted points – some puzzles have lots of points, while occasionally a puzzle has only one. The points become more and more specific the more you read, so reading the first hint will usually give you only a gentle nudge in the direction of what to do. Further hints become progressively more specific, until in some cases you are told how to go about solving the puzzle – but you are never given the full answer. For that you will need the solutions.

SOLUTIONS

The solutions provide two things. First, they do give you the answer to the question as asked, if indeed a question *was* asked – some puzzles simply present content without comment, and it is up to you to work out what is being asked of you! But second, and perhaps more importantly, they show you exactly how you reach that answer, explaining each part of the puzzle in a step-by-step way. This means that even if you initially find the puzzles hard to fathom, if you read through the solutions then you should start to understand how they work.

TWISTED MINDS

The puzzles in this book come from the minds of more than ten different authors, most of whom have considerable experience in setting devious and cryptic challenges, as you can see from their biographies at the back of the book. Sometimes different authors will approach similar puzzle mechanics from very different angles, making sure you are kept on your toes!

Good luck – and have fun!

                                        Gareth Moore, August 2017

Chapter 1
Decipherable

Alan Turing worked on many
different projects throughout
his life, with perhaps his
most famous legacies being
the invention of the Turing
Machine, the Turing Test
and of course his critical
codebreaking work during the
Second World War. Luckily, the
puzzles in this chapter are
considerably easier to crack
than the challenges Turing
faced during the War, but,
even so, you will still find
some challenging enigmas on the
pages that follow.

① FLOWER POWER   *NAME of FLOWERS*

In what way can the following sentences be said to contain flowery language?

▶ A sparkling diamond for the debonair is the height of fashion

▶ Skilled jewel-cutters shape onyx with tools

▶ Lapis lazuli lack the wide range of hues found in other jewels

▶ Euros enable the purchase of German garnets

▶ A gem-buying agenda is yjelding high profits

② MOVIE EDITS   *ANAGRAM*

The following short phrases each represent a well-known film title. Work out how, and then reveal them all.

▶ Oh, fat true bucket!   *BACK TO The fUTURE*

▶ Wed? Nothing white   *GONE with The wind*

▶ Chill 'n distress   *SCHINDLERS LIST*

▶ Angry, invasive trap   *SAVING PRIVATE RYAN*

▶ Performs gut   *FORREST GUMP*

③ WORD CONNECTIONS

There are three words missing in the diagram below. Can you complete it so that all pairs of touching words form a word when joined together?

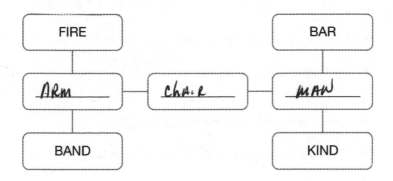

FIRE — ARM — CHAIR — MAN — BAR

BAND

KIND

④ END OF SERIES

What is the final letter in this series? S

▶ T S E L R N S

⑤ WHAT THE...?

The following characters have all been manipulated in the same way. Given the same treatment, what would the author's name look like?

▶ Llts   S

▶ Srggj   N

▶ Skrb   K

▶ Tswt   C

▶ Kcwkcp   D

▶ Hctwgm

(6) CLOCK SCHEDULING

USEING MILITARY TIME 24hR clock

Given the following, what time would Loos represent?

BATTLE of ↓

▶ Britain = twenty to eight in the evening *1940*

▶ Waterloo = quarter past six in the evening ~~1745~~ *1815*

▶ Berlin = quarter to eight in the evening *1945*

▶ Loos = _____ *1915*

(7) COMPLETE THE PICTURE

What is missing from each entry?

▶ D*ollywood*/USA

▶ N*ollywood* Nigeria

▶ B*ollywood* India

▶ H*ollywood* USA

(8) PUNAGRAMS I

Solve the anagrams below to reveal six European countries.
However, each anagram has one extra letter that isn't used.
In order, these read to give an answer to this question:

Which European country do athletes dislike?

▶ BIG MULES   *BELGIUM*   — S

▶ PURE SLAB   *BELARUS*   — P

▶ LINED CAR   *ICELAND*   — R

▶ OVEN ALIAS   *SLOVENIA*   — A

▶ NEW SIDE   *SWEDEN*   — I

▶ BRAISEN   *SERBIA*   — N

9 TETRA-DROP GRID FILL

Drop the tetromino pieces into the grid in the order given so as to spell out ten six-letter words. The pieces may not be rotated or reflected, and must be able to be dropped into the grid from the top so that they come to rest on either another piece or the grid bottom.

V	A	C	A	T	E
B	R	:	S	h	T
M	U	f	f	I N	N
I	S	L	A	N	d
C	O	f	f	E	E
Z	o	m	b	:	A
S	P	:	d	E	R
C	H	A	R	g	E
B	o	T	T	L	E
S	P	R	i	N	T

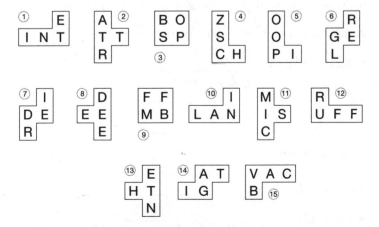

(10) ANAGRAM CONNECTIONS I

Unscramble the following words and find a word that connects them. Note that although some words have more than one anagram, only one of these will fit the connecting word.

- CORNLOT   *CROWD CONTROL*
- ROVE   *OVER CROWED*
- DUFN   *CROWD-FUND*
- NI   *IN CROWD*
- ELAPSING   *CROWD PLEASING*
- COURSE   *CROWD SOURCE*
- FIGURNS   *CROWD SURFING*
- TI   *IT CROWD*
- DINGDAM   *MADDING CROWD*

(11) TABLE OF RIVERS

Which river could follow next in this list?

H

- Humber (1)   *HYDROGEN*

HE

- Hebron (2)   *HELIUM*

Li

- Liffey (3)   *LITHIUM*

BE

- Beaulieu (4)   *BERYLLIUM*

B

- Brahmaputra (5)   *BORON*

C   *CARBON*

⑫ QUOTE HANJIE

Shade in squares in the grid to reveal a picture. Numbers at the start of each row or column reveal, in order from left to right or top to bottom, the length of each consecutive run of shaded squares. There must be a gap of at least one empty square between each run of shaded squares in the same row or column.

Once you have identified and shaded all of the correct squares, the remaining letters will spell out an inspiring quote from Alan Turing.

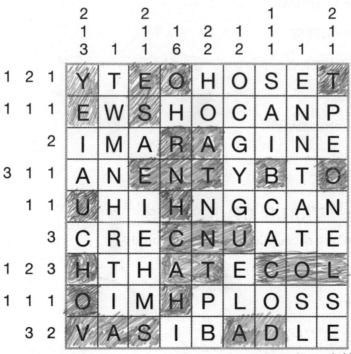

	2 1 3	1	1	2 1 6	1 2 2	1 2	1 1 1	1	2 1 1
1 2 1	Y	T	E	O	H	O	S	E	T
1 1 1	E	W	S	H	O	C	A	N	P
2	I	M	A	R	A	G	I	N	E
3 1 1	A	N	E	N	T	Y	B	T	O
1 1	U	H	I	H	N	G	C	A	N
3	C	R	E	C	N	U	A	T	E
1 2 3	H	T	H	A	T	E	C	O	L
1 1 1	O	I	M	H	P	L	O	S	S
3 2	V	A	S	I	B	A	D	L	E

Those WHo CAN IMAGINE ANYThing CAN CREAT THE IMpossibLE

(13) PUNAGRAMS 2

Solve the anagrams below to reveal seven chemical elements. However, each anagram has one extra letter that isn't used. In order, these read to give an answer to this question:

What is a doctor's most-preferred element?

▶ CHOPPER   _COPPER_   _ H

▶ ORANGE   _ARGON_   _ E

▶ COIN SAIL   _Silicon_   _ A

▶ IS MOULD   _Sodium_   _ L

▶ EVIL SIR   _Silver_   _ I

▶ UNIT   _Tin_   _ U

▶ MEDAL   _Lead_   _ M

(14) COMMON FEATURES I

What is the common feature of all of these words and phrases?   SPORTS

▶ Choice key   Ice Hockey

▶ Tall kebabs   Basketball

▶ North tail   Triathlon

▶ Nine battles   Table Tennis

▶ Hear cry   Archery

▶ A mint bond   Badminton

(15) ANAGRAM CONNECTIONS 2

Unscramble the following words and find a word that connects them. Note that although some words have more than one anagram, only one will fit the connecting word.

▶ CANED *DANCE* *FLOOR*

▶ AES *SEA*

▶ BROAD *FLOOR BOARD*

▶ LAPN *PLANE*

▶ RIFTS *FIRST*

▶ POSH *Shop*

▶ DARTING *TRADING*

▶ PALM *LAMP*

▶ CIPER *PRICE*

(16) ODD NAME OUT I

Which of Oscar's friends is the odd one out?

MOVIE TITLES

▶ Gigi

▶ Hugo — *NO ACADEMY AWARD*

▶ Marty

▶ Oliver

▶ Rebecca

(17) COMMON FEATURES 2

Can you derive a common language feature of all of these
words? What is your reference? Where are you coming from?

Swedish - origin

▶ Moped

▶ Ombudsman

▶ Orienteering

▶ Tungsten

(18) THE VAULT

Mentally revolve the two inner disks until eight four-letter
words are lined up. Each word will begin with the central E
and read outwards in a radial line.

ECHO EARL ENVY EXAM ETCH EWER EASY

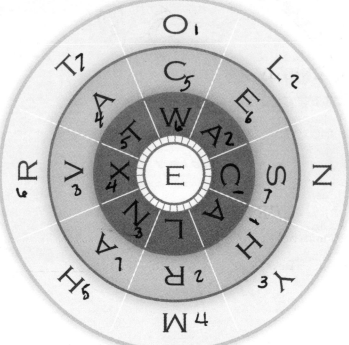

(19) WHERE AM I?

What do all of the following represent, and what property connects them?

- SESESESESESESESESE *TENNESSEE*
- OILLIS *ILLINOIS*

-  *Rhode Island*

- M
  TANA *MONTANA*

- PRIME HASH *NEW HAMPSHIRE*

-  100 kg *WASHINGTON*

-  *PENNSYLVANIA*

- AINIGRIV *WEST VERGINIA*

- I 〰〰〰 CUT *CONNECTICUT*

(20) WATCH THIS

Complete the following calculation:

(Ronin – Days Later) × Angry Men – Hours = _____

DALMATIANS

$$(47-28) \times 12 - 127 = 101$$

(21) COMMON FEATURES 3

What is the common feature of all of these words and phrases?

▶ Apology

▶ Back up

▶ Draw the curtains

▶ Dust

▶ Presently

▶ Sanction

(22) CAN YOU CONNECT I

How can you connect the following words?

▶ Clock

▶ System

▶ Traffic

▶ Egg

▶ Retreat

▶ Drum

(23) ALTERNATIVE EXPRESSIONS I

Can you re-express each of these phrases?

▶ A palm's robin has double the value of a shrub robin

▶ A destiny worse than an ending

▶ Well known for 900 seconds

▶ A sharp pain in the side, that's punctual, rescues just under ten

▶ Tear up because lactose has pooled on the floor

▶ Trout on land

(24) ANAGRAM CONNECTIONS 3

Unscramble the following words and find a word that connects them. Note that although some words have more than one anagram, only one will fit the connecting word.

▶ TREAF

▶ AKTECJ

▶ GHHI

▶ ITEM

▶ FALH

▶ DISZE

▶ DOBOL

▶ LAYFIM

▶ CLEYC

▶ DARGU

㉕ SIX MIX I

There are six six-letter anagrammable words in the first of the following grids. A seventh word, LAPTOP, can be read in the marked diagonal.

Rearrange the six words into six new words, and place them into the second grid in such a way that the word PURPLE occupies the diagonal shaded squares.

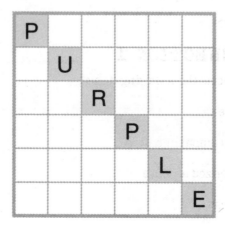

(26) COMMON FEATURES 4

What is the common feature of all of these words and phrases?

▶ Irk angel (4,4)

▶ Crisp eel (8)

▶ The woman's the fighter (3,6,2,3,5)

▶ The footman's in (5,2,6)

▶ Dilute major one (5,3,6)

(27) KEY NUMBERS

If !)) is a ton, ((is a type of ice cream, !*!% is Waterloo,))& is a fictional spy and ^^^ is satanic, what would (!! mean, in the US?

(28) CONNECTION I

What connects the following items?

▶ Cafetière

▶ Salad accompaniment

▶ Unauthorized absence

▶ Eggy bread

▶ Chips

(29) LITERARY SET

Can you identify what category of things is being referenced in the same way in the following titles of literary works?

▶ The Murder Road

▶ H is for Kettle

▶ The Parliament and the Pussycat

▶ The Maltese Cast

▶ The Wings of the Flight

▶ Where Convocations Dare

▶ Wild Bevies

▶ Flaubert's Company

▶ Shroud for a Watch

(30) MOVIE CLUB I

Can you identify the correct movie titles and deduce what principle is being applied?

▶ Charlie Harding's War

▶ King Cleveland

▶ The Eisenhower Show

▶ Get Reagan

▶ Jeremiah Nixon

(31) OBSCENE TITLES

Can you identify the correct titles and work out the way in which they have been altered?

▶ Aegean's Eleven

▶ Electric Magnolias

▶ The True Tenenbaums

▶ Navy Grit

▶ Royal Kool-Aid Acid Test

▶ Baby in Wonderland

(32) MOVIE CLUB 2

Can you identify the correct movie titles and deduce what principle is being applied?

▶ Jackie Blair

▶ East of Churchill

▶ Major Witch Project

▶ Fifty Shades of Wellington

▶ Thatcher Dundee

▶ Fitzroy by Fitzroy West

(33) PUNAGRAMS 3

Solve the anagrams below to reveal seven flowers. However, each anagram has one extra letter that isn't used. In order, these read to give an answer to this question:

What flowers can you find on your face? (3-4)

▶ THAI LAD   _____ __

▶ CROW HID   _____ __

▶ OUR ENIGMA   _____ __

▶ LIT LOVE   _____ __

▶ RAINS OFF   _____ __

▶ CAMEL SPIT   _____ __

▶ SILLY   _____ __

(34) RADICAL TITLES

Can you identify the correct titles and identify the way in which they have been altered?

▶ Blood Tuesday

▶ Rose Tide

▶ A Study in Berry

▶ The Wine Orchard

▶ Lipstick Lane

35 NAVIGRID I

Place the digits 1 to 9 so that it is possible to jump from one digit to the next, in consecutive order, using the steps provided. Each step is an instruction to move a number of squares horizontally and/or vertically, and each must be used exactly once, in an order of your choosing. No part of a step can involve crossing over a black square.

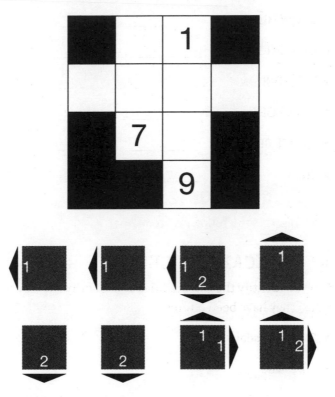

36 AGENT ACTIVITY

What word is created by linking Dracula, Ireland in poetic form, a Swiss hero, iodine, information and the Anglican church?

(37) LATELY LONGING

Can you complete the final entry in this list?

▶ 0 = Gulf of Guinea

▶ 15 = Chad

▶ 30 = Egypt

▶ 45 = Russia

▶ 60 = Russia

▶ 75 = Kara Sea

▶ 90 = _____

(38) CONNECTION 2

What connects the following items?

▶ Slander

▶ A Muslim woman's headdress

▶ Informal refusal

▶ Wall plaster

▶ Pacific Ocean island territory

(39) TRAVEL TEST

If you found Open Change in Denmark, Sandwich Tong in the USA, and Armed Mats in the Netherlands, what 'greater' thing might you find in Italy?

(40) FEATURE I

Can you identify the common feature of the following words?

▶ Half

▶ Salmon

▶ Yolk

▶ Balm

▶ Would

▶ Chalk

(41) SWAP AND SWITCH

Answer the first clue by replacing one letter from the word SECRET with a different letter, then rearranging the letters – and keep track of the new letter using the column to the right. Do the same again for each of the subsequent clues, replacing one letter from the previous answer in each case until you have answered all the clues. Finally, unscramble the 'new' letters to reveal another word.

                                         S E C R E T

▶ Restrictive undergarment   _ _ _ _ _ _   _

▶ Association football   _ _ _ _ _ _   _

▶ Cut with shallow lines   _ _ _ _ _ _   _

▶ Small unit of time   _ _ _ _ _ _   _

▶ Trigonometry function   _ _ _ _ _ _   _

▶ Elegantly groomed   _ _ _ _ _ _   _

(42) GLOBETROTTING I

I've been driving around the US recently. Can you decode the hidden message in each trip I make?

▶ What kind of tourist attraction might I visit on the following trip?
Augusta > Jefferson City > Providence > Montgomery

▶ What will I do when I get home from this trip?
Boulder > Tulsa > Lewiston > Birmingham

▶ What is the first thing I will do when I arrive back from this next trip?
Dover > Boston > Fargo > Madison > Lincoln

▶ Where did all these trips take place? My final journey was:
Cape Cod > Fort Wayne > New Orleans > Grand Forks

▶ What greeting did I therefore avoid on my travels?

(43) FEATURE 2

What common feature do all of the following words share?

▶ Muscle

▶ Scissors

▶ Ascent

▶ Miscellaneous

▶ Scenario

(44) ALPHAHUNT I

This wordsearch grid contains some hidden words, all at least four letters long, which can be written in any direction, either forwards or backwards, including diagonally. For the purposes of this puzzle, ignore any words of fewer than four letters. Once you have found the words, you will notice that every letter of the alphabet has been used at least once – except one. Which is that unused letter?

```
B A Z T R A U Q H T
P U G K A E I B G C
E W R I N K L E I H
C X M G Y H S K U A
N J E A L O U S Y R
E O D R T A D W F G
L T I E C Y R I Y E
O W U U N I F O R M
I E M A O U S P W V
V F P P O B P E K D
```

A B C D E F G H I J K L M N O P Q R S T U V W X Y Z

(45) IN OTHER WORDS

Miss Poppins had a small sheep with milky wool, and it accompanied her to each place she went. Where did she take it first?

(46) CAN YOU CONNECT 2

How can you connect the following words?

▶ Exam

▶ Fire

▶ Clock

▶ Date

▶ Trap

▶ Reminder

▶ Table

(47) SPOT THE LINK I

Can you identify the link between the following words?

▶ Abbot

▶ Almost

▶ Bellow

▶ Chintz

▶ Efflux

▶ Flossy

(48) SIX MIX 2

There are six six-letter, anagrammable words in the first of the following grids. A seventh word, SECRET, can be read in the marked diagonal.

Rearrange the six words into six new words, and place them into the second grid in such a way that the word TEMPLE occupies the diagonal shaded squares.

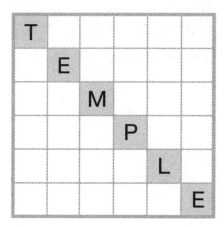

(49) SPOT THE LINK 2

Can you identify the link between the following words?

▶ August

▶ Contract

▶ Intimate

▶ Invalid

▶ Object

▶ Polish

▶ Present

▶ Recreation

▶ Sewer

▶ Tear

(50) CAN YOU CONNECT 3

How can you connect the following words?

▶ Cold

▶ Train

▶ Ball

▶ Break

▶ Fish

▶ Thief

(51) REBUSES

What do each of the following represent, and what connects them?

▶

▶ RO   PE

▶ 3333333333333333333333333333333333333333

▶ BLEMISH + IF + EYE

▶ B
  O
  X

▶ EVER ~~E~~

▶ ST RAM AG

(52) STRIP SEARCH

Can you complete this story?

▶ First, I was a band of buccaneers on the high seas

▶ Then, I was angry

▶ Next, I was a rodent that is often considered a pest

▶ Finally, I was _____

(53) MUSIC MIX

Can you identify each of the following original music tracks, before they were re-mixed?

▶ Also a Salt Bathtub – Rather Moaning

▶ Angered – Mourns Bar

▶ I Dislike Rags – Perky Tray

▶ Sack by Ex – Junk Albeit Merits

▶ A Vivid Lava – Dopy Call

▶ House of Pay – Hears Need

▶ Wail Lively As You Low – Why Shout In Tone

(54) SPORTS FILL

Place all of these Olympic sports into the grid, one letter per box. The shaded squares will then spell out a sport new to the 2020 Summer Olympics in Tokyo.

ARCHERY	HOCKEY
ATHLETICS	JUDO
BADMINTON	RUGBY
BASKETBALL	SAILING
BOXING	SWIMMING
DIVING	TENNIS
FENCING	TRAMPOLINE
FOOTBALL	TRIATHLON
GOLF	VOLLEYBALL
HANDBALL	WATER POLO

(55) GEM OF A PUZZLE

I'm needed for curling, and I am many a pound.

I can be a punishment, and I'm seen on the ground.

But get me in the kidneys, and pain will be found.

What am I?

(56) CAPITAL LETTERS

Where am I going?

▶ Low budget film   _ - _ _ _ _ _

▶ A sudden reversal in decision   _ - _ _ _ _

▶ 6th June 1944   _ - _ _ _

▶ Very famous person   _ - _ _ _ _ _ _

▶ Bent pipe under a sink   _ - _ _ _ _

▶ Region of ionosphere that reflects   _ - _ _ _ _ _
  medium frequency radio waves

▶ Fast German railway line   _ - _ _ _ _

▶ Casually worn top   _ - _ _ _ _ _

(57) ONE MORE LETTER

With the addition of one more letter, each word can be rearranged to answer the clues. Find all ten correct answers and your new letters will spell out the surname of a famous classical composer.

▶ TALE _____ Fewest

▶ ROSE _____ Shop

▶ TOGA _____ Medieval coin

▶ RIND _____ Water outlet

▶ LATE _____ Butler

▶ SPAR _____ European capital

▶ PIES _____ Backbone

▶ CAPE _____ Room to move

▶ COST _____ Meat broth

▶ SEAR _____ Periods of time

(58) LINK WORDS

Find a word which can go in the middle of each line to create two further words – one when combined with the preceding word, and another when combined with the following word:

▶ WASTE _____ BALL

▶ SAW _____ BIN

▶ BED _____ SHEET

▶ EAR _____ TICK

▶ CON _____ ANT

(59) LATIN PAIRS

Complete each grid so as to avoid any repeats within the same row or column, using KLMTVW in the first grid and 123456 in the second grid. Then, add the numbers in the shaded squares to the letters in the matching shaded squares (e.g. A + 3 = D) to get six new letters. Rearrange these letters to reveal the name of a country.

	K		M		
		T		V	
W		L		V	
K		M		W	T
	V		M		L

	2	6		3	
3			4	1	
5					
	3	5		2	1
		4			3
	6		1	4	5

(60) DROP ZONE

You have seven stacks of lettered balls. Remove a ball and the others above it will drop down in its place. Your task is to remove one ball from each column so that when all the other balls drop down, they will spell out six words reading across.

Which balls should you remove, and what word will be spelled out by them?

Chapter 2
Computable

At a time when computers were in their infancy, Turing helped formalize the concept of a computable algorithm by inventing the Turing Machine, a simple, hypothetical machine which is capable of simulating any logical algorithm, no matter how complicated. Unlike other models of computation, Turing's was accessible and intuitive. Find out how creative and intuitive you can be too, with the more challenging puzzles in this second chapter.

(I) GOING IN BLIND

Solve the clues below and then fill the grid with the answers.
To help, the solutions to the clues will be in alphabetical
order when correctly solved.

▶ Finger, for instance (5)   _____

▶ Country in the South Pacific (4)   _____

▶ The end of a race (6)   _____

▶ Very cold (6)   _____

▶ Thumbing a lift from place to place (5-6)   _____

▶ Something unstated but suggested (8)   _____

▶ A period in baseball (6)   _____

▶ Part of the eye (4)   _____

▶ A New Zealander, or one of its birds (4)   _____

▶ Extremely angry (5)   _____

▶ Words in a song (6)   _____

▶ Half note, equal to two crotchets (5)   _____

▶ US state (11)   _____

▶ Informal outdoor meal (6)   _____

▶ Someone on a religious journey (7)   _____

▶ An edible decapod (6)   _____

▶ Apple's helper (4)   _____

▶ Winter sport (6)   _____

▶ Shy (5)   _____

▶ Book series by Stephenie Meyer (8)   _____

▶ Casualty (6)   _____

▶ Richard Branson's brand (6)   _____

② PIVOT POINTS

What unusual property do the following words all share?

▶ MAD

▶ ROT

▶ TEN

▶ DEW

▶ SAG

▶ LEV

③ HOLY ORDERS

Place these confused entries into order:

▶ Burns me

▶ No remedy out

▶ Ex duos

▶ See sign

▶ Cut is vile

④ MAN TO MAN

Can you join each pair of men by inserting two words so that each pair of adjacent words are synonyms? For example, you could join TAIL to COPY with TAIL > SHADOW > TRACE > COPY.

▶ ROB   >   ____   >   ____   >   JOSH

▶ PAT   >   ____   >   ____   >   MIDGE

▶ NICK   >   ____   >   ____   >   JOHN

▶ MARK   >   ____   >   ____   >   BILL

⑤ A NEW TERM

Some children were sent to school – which one?

6 8 9 2 3 8 8 9 7 1 4 5 2 1 8 3 1 9

(6) CAN YOU CONNECT 4

How can you connect the following words?

▶ Blood

▶ Dagger

▶ Curtains

▶ Bath

▶ Picture

▶ Audience

▶ Conclusion

(7) ROUTE SUM

If you take away the common denominator in these events, but add their remaining parts, what sum would you obtain?

▶ Battle of Hastings

▶ Death of William the Bad of Sicily

▶ Battle of Benevento

▶ The Statutes of Kilkenny

▶ Death of Donatello

▶ Murder of David Rizzio in the Palace of Holyroodhouse

▶ Great Fire of London

▶ Britain's repeal of the Stamp Act

▶ Austro-Prussian War

▶ The Beatles' last live concert (that took place in San Francisco)

⑧ NAVIGRID 2

Place the digits 1 to 9 so that it is possible to jump from one digit to the next, in consecutive order, using the steps provided. Each step is an instruction to move a number of squares horizontally and/or vertically, and each must be used exactly once, in an order of your choosing. No part of a step can involve crossing over a black square.

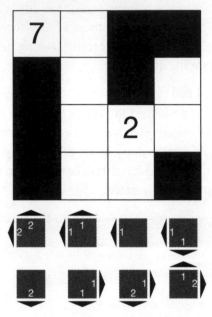

⑨ MISFORTUNE

The following items have a common feature to deduce:

▶ Millard Fillmore

▶ Lace

▶ I Chronicles

▶ Fra Mauro area, on the first attempt

▶ Abolition of slavery

▶ Ophiuchus

(10) ENDEAVOUR TO SOLVE

Decode the following message to identify a secret password:

Dear Sarah,

Your letters have been an excellent antidote to the poor weather in dreary London! I apologize for my own responses being so slapdash: I haven't had much time for casual correspondence lately, but don't think me any less doting than ever! Still, after much ado there's finally been some progress here, and I'm hoping it won't be long before we're ready to sign on the dotted line...

I'm very sorry I had to dash Jimmy's hopes about helping with the science project – I'm sure he'll manage just fine without dada's help though nonetheless, and hopefully you won't be driven too dotty in the process! If you're after something a bit spectacular, a dash of vinegar in some baking soda shouldn't go amiss.

Anyway, I've got to be at King's Cross at twelve on the dot, so I'd better dash...

Eternally Yours,

James

(11) ODD NAME OUT 2: VENGEANCE

Which of these fictional characters is the odd one out?

▶ Steve

▶ Natasha

▶ Clint

▶ Scott

▶ Tony

(12) ELEPHANT DEVICES

The following mnemonics are used for remembering
particular sequences. Can you identify them from their
components? In some cases the sentence gives a hint to the
nature of the sequence.

▶ Every Good Boy Deserves Fun

▶ My Very Eager Mother Just Served Us Nine Pizzas

▶ Bring Your Record Breaking Guy/Girl

▶ God's Eternal Love Never Dies

▶ Super Heroes Must Eat Oats

▶ Tall Girls Can Fight and Other Queer Things Can Develop

▶ Charmingly Nubile Ladies Mollify Debonair British
Commander

(13) HIDDEN FLOWERS

Can you detect the five flowers hidden in the following
passage?

Kew Gardens is a beloved place to stop off to see flowers
from across the world. It always provides fantastic
amusement to see the exotic names and variety of species.
There have been many new ones placed into the collection,
I learn. Even the most zealous enthusiast for flowers
would have their interests satisfied. One can find useful
information everywhere and some people concoct a gushing
tribute at the end of their visit.

(14) PISCINE PHRASES

▶ The following statements contain 'fishy' elements. In some cases, the incidence occurs more than once. Can you find all thirteen?

▶ It's insupportable a king should abdicate when under pressure

▶ There's no desire in the general population for a long-forgotten church

▶ Toys termed intelligence elements are developed or yet to be used in other rings for spying operations

▶ Tourists escape lines in busy coastal port

▶ The lack of foreign languages in British education is a basic oddity

▶ People stop outside for drinkable treats

▶ All kinds of money emanate easily from a rich aristocrat

(15) FEATURE 3

Can you identify the common feature of the following words?

▶ Handkerchief

▶ Wednesday

▶ Adjust

▶ Handsome

(16) FOUR BY FOUR I

Solve the clues and fit their answers into the 4×4 grid, so they read either across or down. Each answer is four letters long. To make things trickier, the clues are given in no particular order. One letter is already filled in.

- ▶ Now! (initials)

- ▶ Lids

- ▶ Counts at a gym

- ▶ Reduce difficulty

- ▶ Ensnare

- ▶ Badger's home

- ▶ A-lister, for example

- ▶ Tropical plant with edible root

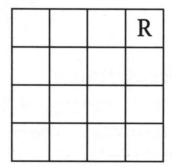

(17) TABLE OF COUNTRIES

Which country could follow next in this list?

- ▶ Albania (13)

- ▶ Singapore (14)

- ▶ Philippines (15)

18 KLUMP I

Shade some circles so that the remaining numbers are joined together into groups of one, two or three circles. The sum of the numbers in each group must match one of the totals provided. Each total is used exactly once. Groups may not touch each other, and neither may shaded circles.

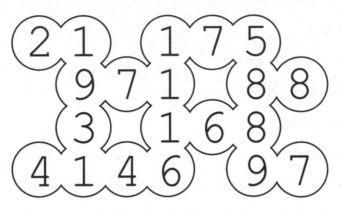

Totals: 5 6 7 9 12 22

19 GLOBETROTTING 2

Follow this journey, and answer the questions.

▶ I went to Casablanca, Vilnius and Vienna. Which island state did I visit after that?

▶ Then I went to Lisbon, Seville and Bujumbura. Which South American country was next on my itinerary?

▶ I saw Rome and visited Buenos Aires, then flew to Doha. Which Arab state did I go on to?

▶ And what did I say before setting off for Venice, Lagos, Bangkok, Nuku'alofa, Istanbul, Salzburg, Vatican City, Madrid, Luxembourg, Torshavn, Buenos Aires, Tblisi and Stockholm?

20 VENN I

Can you identify the rule used to sort the elements in this
Venn diagram?

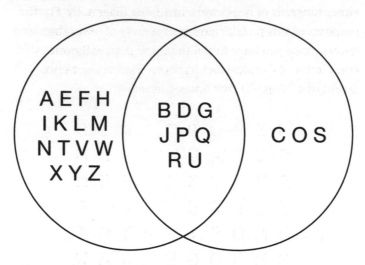

21 PUNAGRAMS 4

Solve the anagrams below to reveal six types of dog.
However, each anagram has two extra letters that aren't
used. In order, these read to give an answer to this question,
but note that the two leftover letters from each clue could
be either way around:

What is a dog's most-loved movie? (8,4)

▶ TREES JUT   _____   _ _

▶ ADORES YAM   _____   _ _

▶ DUNGY HORSES   _____   _ _

▶ CANADA LIMIT   _____   _ _

▶ APE BLOOD   _____   _ _

▶ BREAK LEG   _____   _ _

(22) ALPHAHUNT 2

This wordsearch grid contains some hidden words, all at least four letters long, which can be written in any direction, either forwards or backwards, including diagonally. For the purposes of this puzzle, ignore any words of fewer than four letters. Once you have found the words, you will notice that every letter of the alphabet has been used at least once – except one. Which is that unused letter?

```
W Y B O P C F W I H
C U T A U I K Y A M
D Y E T Z B L E U M
E G D O E O U L O A
U M O S I R R I O I
E M S Q G E P J A W
U H N U P A T E X T
F N O I T C A R F I
I D V S P I F K L Y
F W K H S A N G B U
```

A B C D E F G H I J K L M N O P Q R S T U V W X Y Z

(23) ALWAYS ASK WHY

The result is missing from the final soccer match. What was the score, and why?

▶ Manchester City   1   0   Manchester United

▶ Derby County   2   1   Crystal Palace

▶ Liverpool   0   2   York City

▶ Plymouth Argyle   ___   ___   Grimsby Town

(24) WHO'S NEXT?

The following names are arranged in a specific sequence.
Enter an appropriate name in the empty last position.

▶ Bush

▶ Shakespeare

▶ Beckham

▶ Scissorhands

▶ Clooney

▶ Norton

▶ Harrison

▶ _____

(25) FEATURE 4

Can you identify the common feature of the following
words?

▶ Castle

▶ Christmas

▶ Listen

▶ Often

▶ Hasten

▶ Rapport

▶ Gourmet

▶ Ballet

26 WALL TO WALL

The answers to these clues zigzag back and forth across the grid, changing direction with each new line. The last letter of one answer is the first of the next. When you've finished, the shaded diagonal will spell out a mystery word.

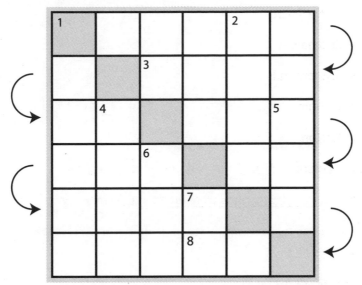

1. Continental quilt (5)
2. Garden songbird (6)
3. African canine carnivore (5)
4. Plant that gives liquorice its taste (5)
5. Land of Hope and Glory composer (5)
6. Sporting arbiter (7)
7. Stamp a design into paper (6)
8. Male deer (4)

27 OBSCURE

I need water to form but I might give it back,

And I'm back up for you when your gadgets crack.

What am I?

(28) NEXT LINE

What comes next in the following lyrical sequence?

▸ 5GR

▸ 4CB

▸ 3FH

▸ 2TD

(29) WORD FUNKTION

Can you identify the common link in the following?

▸ Excess weight gained from emotional overeating

▸ The feeling that time is running out for opportunities as one gets older

▸ Distance-sickness – a longing for far-off places

▸ A strong desire to travel

▸ Malicious enjoyment of someone else's misfortunes

(30) MUDDIED TITLES

Can you identify the correct titles and the way in which they have been altered?

▸ Under Milk Chocolate

▸ Cinnamon Cantata

▸ Charlie Russet

▸ Charlie and the Chestnut Factory

(31) DOUBLE DUTY NAMES

The following nine capital cities can be divided into two groups of five. Which one is doing double duty?

▶ Athens

▶ Bamako

▶ Budapest

▶ Buenos Aires

▶ Copenhagen

▶ Islamabad

▶ Kigali

▶ Ottawa

▶ Sucre

(32) IT'S ALL AN ACT

Can you name the actor?

▶ Cuddly	_____	poodle
▶ Fairy	_____	teller
▶ Think	_____	apple
▶ Energy	_____	grace
▶ In	_____	investigator
▶ Meg	_____	Gosling
▶ Storm	_____	nine
▶ Road	_____	mountains

33 QUESTION

Use your word interrogation skills to decide what each of these six entries is hiding. Once fully revealed, two of them will be anagrams of one another.

▶ H

▶ H

▶ HA

▶ HE

▶ HER

▶ O

34 DEPARTURES

One of the destinations is missing from this airport departure board. If you take your time, you can count on the destination to help you find the missing departure. What is it?

Departure	Time
Brussels	13:15
Melbourne	21:30
New York	06:10
Kuala Lumpur	04:05
Rio De Janeiro	09:15
Copenhagen	18:25
Antananarivo	19:30
Cairo	17:20
Hong Kong	05:10

(35) CAESAR'S FINAL MOVE

'Et tu, Brute!' Caesar exclaimed, as he saw his murderer bearing down on him on the Ides of March. But which of the following suspects was it? They all look shifty.

▶ O P N Zop

▶ N T Aspc

▶ H Z Cod

▶ P E E F McFep

▶ P Yuzj

(36) ECOLOGICAL TITLES

Can you identify the correct titles and detect the way in which they have been altered?

▶ Parsley Avocado Rosemary and Thyme

▶ Neon Express

▶ Islamic Texas

▶ Moss Tiger

▶ Key Mint Pie

(37) NUMERACY

In an old numeracy test, the following scores were obtained. If Tammi had competed, what would she have scored?

▶ Alan scored 50

▶ Kevin scored 6

▶ Clive scored 154

(38) EVER-DECREASING CIRCLES

Visit every circle. What's the path?

START Years in a century	L	Single RPM	Steps	Strikes in three perfect games in bowling
Distance to the target in Olympic archery (m)	Squares on a checkered boardgame	The answer to Life, the Universe and Everything	Winks in a nap	FDR
Bryan Adams' Summer	Eleventh triangular number	Circles in this puzzle	Hendrix, Joplin and Winehouse's 'Club'	Days in four months?
First number with four 'E's	Noble gas group	Spots on a dice	Cats' Lives	Golf warning?
Sweet	3x3 magic square constant	Stripes on a US flag	German 'no'?	US international dial code

(39) STEPPING WITH STYLE

These puzzles make it seem like you take one step forward and then two steps back!

▶ VJHEG FZPBG LGZPR 'FNWAND-USGO' KM UOCMKRJ?

(40) TANGLED DUOS

Untangle each pair of related items. The letters in each pair are in the correct order for each item, but the items can be mixed in any way.

For example, WBLHACITKE = BLACK and WHITE

▶ SAPEPPELTR

▶ SCHONNERY

▶ JUROLIMETEO

▶ QUKIENENG

▶ BUBTREATEDR

▶ HARMMODERGESTERINS

▶ MISKSEPIRGMIGTY

▶ GADOBBALNACE

▶ BARTOBINMAN

▶ EADAVEM

▶ CANTLEOHOPANTRAY

▶ BETAHEUBETASTY

▶ POCALLSTORUX

▶ MALUIRIGIO

▶ PETELNLERN

(41) HEADS OF STATE

My first was the first, looking straight ahead.
My second was actually third, looking to his left.
My third was twenty-sixth, looking even further left.
Who is my fourth and final?

(42) SAVAGE BRACKETS

Can you complete the missing words?

		_____	BOY
			SHOW
			THEORY
			BAIT
	_____	_____	FIN
			TANK
			FOOTBALL
		_____	SALT
			MANNERS
			FIELD
		_____	OUT
			MAJEUR
			FRAUD
_____	_____	_____	POLICY
			AGENT
			FICTION
		_____	PARK
			MUSEUM
			MOUSE
		_____	TRIP
			HOCKEY
			TRAIL
	_____	_____	BAG
			CLIP
			MIX
		_____	WALK
			TIN

(43) SUPERMARKET SHENANIGANS

I went into the supermarket and bought 33 BANANAs, 50 MANGOs and 40 PEARs. How many APPLEs did I buy?

(44) VENN 2

Can you identify the rule used to sort the elements in this Venn diagram?

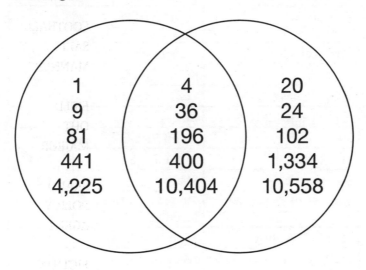

(45) A STARTING CODE IS INVOLVED

Can you de-hex these characters?

57　　65　　6C　　63　　6F　　6D　　65

(46) DEPECHE CODE

My friend, a keen puzzle-setter, handed me this CD and said:
'When I can't solve a music puzzle, I think of doing this.'
What does he do?

TRACK	ARTIST	LENGTH
Isn't She Lovely	Stevie Wonder	1:38
Night Fever	Bee Gees	5:23
Dynamite	Taio Cruz	5:20
Eye of the Tiger	Survivor	7:29
Xanadu	Olivia Newton-John & ELO	7:34
American Pie	Madonna	3:35
Ruby	Kaiser Chiefs	4:36
Three Times A Lady	Commodores	3:18
If You Leave Me Now	Chicago	3:26
Sorry	Justin Bieber	6:36
The Reflex	Duran Duran	7:34
Boombastic	Shaggy	1:20
You've Got The Love	Florence and the Machine	1:16
Man In The Mirror	Michael Jackson	2:19
I'd Do Anything For Love (But I Won't Do That)	Meat Loaf	8:20
Never Gonna Give You Up	Rick Astley	7:18
Under Pressure	Queen ft. David Bowie	4:30
The Wonder of You	Elvis Presley	8:19
Everytime	Britney Spears	5:16

(47) FOUR BY FOUR 2

Solve the clues and fit their answers into the 4×4 grid, so they read either across or down. Each answer is four letters long. To make things trickier, the clues are given in no particular order. One letter is already filled in.

▶ V, long ago

▶ Thought

▶ To be, long ago

▶ Bestow

▶ To a smaller extent

▶ Mountain or valley, in origami

▶ Poetry

▶ Go out with

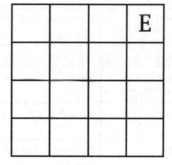

(48) BEEPING MAD

What method of signalling can be found in the middle of the Timor Sea?

(49) SECONDS AND THIRDS

What comes next in each of these sequences?

▶ NE, WO, HR, OU, IV, IX, EV, IG, IN, _____

▶ AT, UN, ON, UE, ED, HU, _____

▶ YD, EL, IT, ER, OR, AR, IT, XY, _____

▶ ED, RA, EL, RE, LU, ND, _____

▶ AS, DA, EF, AD, ON, DA, AC, AN, AR, YL, OL, AY, IL, IE, UC, _____

▶ RI, AU, EM, AN, EO, IR, IB, CO, AG, AP, QU, _____

(50) BACKWORDS

Given the first three examples of a particular relationship, can you complete the unfinished example?

▶ FASTEN becomes ROLES

▶ UNCOOKED becomes HOSTILITY

▶ ANXIOUS becomes PUDDINGS

▶ JEANS MATERIAL becomes _____

(51) SCRATCH THAT

What am I?

▶ I'm essential in the Caribbean

▶ I explain a map

▶ I set the tone for musicians

(52) ON DEAF EARS

What appropriate word are the following words clues to?

▶ Reign

▶ Leopard

▶ Salmon

▶ Handkerchief

▶ Give

▶ Column

(53) MIDDLESIX I

Arrange the letters of the word CENTURION into the empty grid squares to create six five-letter words, three reading across and three reading down.

	F	D	F	
P				E
S				G
C				H
	N	K	E	

(54) COME AGAIN?

Solve each clue to reveal an appropriate phrase.

▶ French dance   ? _ _

▶ Latin American dance   _ _ ?

▶ New York prison   _ _ ? _

▶ Good vision and a form of cricket   _ _ _ _ _ ?

▶ Extinct bird   _ ?

▶ African dish made from semolina   _ _ ? _

▶ Caused by lack of vitamin B1   _ _ ? _

▶ Bloodsucking African fly   _ _ ?

▶ Cheerleading accessory   ? _ _

▶ German spa town   _ _ _ ? _

▶ Musical 'Lady'   _ ?

▶ 'Millionaire' life-line   _ _ _ ? _

▶ Plaque   ? _ _

▶ Hawaiian fish   _ _ ? _

▶ Nickname of both the Pope and Hemingway   _ ?

▶ Drum and sat-nav brand   ? _ _

(55) SO IT BEGINS (AND ENDS)

Can you complete each of these words so that they all repeat the same property?

▶ _ _ UR _ _

▶ _ _ SUL _ _

▶ _ _ ADAC _ _

▶ _ _ BL _ _

▶ _ _ CAP _ _

▶ _ _ G _ _

▶ _ _ HERN _ _

▶ _ _ CI _ _

▶ _ _ OTOGRA _ _

▶ _ _ CKLI _ _

(56) ALTERNATIVE EXPRESSIONS 2

Can you re-express each of these phrases?

▶ An amused wooden part of a gun

▶ Just with four sides of equal length and four right angles

▶ Limping mallard

▶ How to grow lettuce

▶ A savage geometric shape

▶ Turn towards pop, rock or country, for example

(57) SPY LOGIC

Three of the journalists attending an international conference were found to have specially adapted spying equipment disguised as personal belongings. These belongings were an electric toothbrush, a bottle of nail polish and an orange lipstick. MI6 Agent Emma Harrison, working undercover as hotel staff, reported the following:

▶ Kristina Karpova's toothbrush wasn't electric

▶ The camera was found in Ms Zukova's room

▶ The transmitter was in a nail polish bottle

▶ Natalia, who was not Ms Pavlova, had the orange lipstick

Using the grid below as an aid, work out each woman's full name, the spy equipment they were using, and how each gadget was disguised.

	Pavlova	Zukova	Karpova	Toothbrush	Nail polish	Orange lipstick	Transmitter	Flash drive	Camera
Natalia									
Valentina									
Kristina									
Transmitter						
Flash drive						
Camera						
Toothbrush			
Nail polish			
Orange lipstick			

Chapter 3
Testing

In a 1950 paper Turing proposed 'The Imitation Game', a method of judging whether a computer had become 'intelligent', which came to be known as the Turing Test. The test simply states that if a human tester cannot tell the difference between the responses of a machine and the responses of a human, then the machine can be said to be intelligent. It's time now to test your own intelligence, with this chapter of tougher puzzles.

(1) UK TRANSPORT PREDICTIONS

Terms in this chart refer in four different ways to twelve common items in a specific group. One can navigate a way to find four separate categories of three.

BILL	SQUARE
DONOVAN	PHARAOHS
SOUL	DICK
GORGED	BED HIRES
HOE	CARRIE
WHITE	FATTENS

(2) FIVE BY FOUR

Can you group these words, names and phrases to form five non-overlapping sets? Each set will contain exactly four items.

CHESTNUT	FAWN
RUSSET	JAZZ
BLINKY	CHEWY
HOOTER	MUG
FIZZY	NOODLE
DISCOVERY	CHOCOLATE
FUJI	INKY
CLYDE	PINS
PINKY	TAN
BOILED	SOUR

③ THE MAN WITH THE GOLDEN PUN

Identify the following lesser-known motion pictures from these brief descriptions:

▶ You are given something solely for your female sheep

▶ Permission is given for an invoice to be sent

▶ The near future will bring only truth

▶ A scenic window looking over a small mountain

▶ Global warming must be stopped

▶ Perish in a future month

▶ Heirs to the throne who live it up in Las Vegas

▶ A hesitant refusal

▶ There is a limit to how many times you dance

④ NEXT IN LINE I

What should come next in each of the following real-world sequences, and why?

▶   M   V   E   M   J   S

▶   F   S   T   F   F   S

▶   I   V   X   L   C   D

▶   M   A   M   J   J   A

▶   F   S   S   M   T   W

⑤ ESCAPED ANIMALS

Various animals have escaped from the sentences below. Can you restore them all? The number of letters in each animal's name is given after each sentence.

For example: 'Rat' has escaped from 'Came here to take photos' (3); once restored the sentence reads 'Camera there to take photos'.

▶ It's the dolly used to play with my friend (4)

▶ Which sis will be most suitable for modelling in the lingerie department? (5)

▶ Heard woman putting on clothes after bathing (5)

▶ Male beast to finish the race, having fallen first (5)

▶ Is a bully to rise from their bed in the spring? (4)

⑥ DIVERSITY TEST

The following items are in a particular sequence. A final element that continues the sequence is to be deduced.

▶ T H F R O by T C (3,6)

▶ A C O by A B (7,7)

▶ C Y by A H (6,6)

▶ A O G G by L M M (4,4,10)

▶ P B by T S (3,6)

▶ I by A H (5,7)

▶ _____

(7) LIFE FORMS

Transform each word in the first column to make a new word in the second column, using the same transformation method for all rows. Next, transform each word in the second column to make a new word in the third column, again using the same transformation method for all rows (although this will be different from the method used to transform from column one to column two). Each word in the resulting third group will have something in common – what?

DOTE		
ROBE		
KILNS		
ASHORE		
DARE		
TEACHER		

(8) KEY WORDS

In what way might it be considered that the two words 'after-effects' and 'niminy-piminy' are opposite versions of the same phenomenon?

(9) SEQUENCE I

In this sequence, what item might come next?

▶ Big Bend

▶ Carlsbad Caverns

▶ Grand Canyon

(10) HOUSE-HUNTING

A series of common items in chronological order has to be deduced from the text. Each item is referred to by a definition and letter mixture in which the definition may precede or follow an anagram of the word's letters, and the set of letters for each anagram must start at the beginning of a word or finish at the end of a word. One member of the group (4-6-5) is missing and has to be deduced. Some sentences contain more than one item and the definition and letter mixture can appear across multiple sentences.

Wisdom, perhaps, in Roman natives or those given an area of western France is observed. Some get plate annually for Latin sprig of broom? Clear standards are seen from bomber during itinerary – OK. Bowl in stadium tour demonstrates a fine architectural style. Little, perhaps, found in a trust putting fruit on great display. Hear novel German city has left Barbara, maybe, struggling to react in words.

(11) FINAL AGENT

Which four-word movie title can be deduced from the following?

▶ A, o, out, re

▶ Brig, err, rib, thous

▶ Gob, leaf, pal, tab

▶ Bad, cad, foo, in

(12) WORD ASSOCIATION

Complete the missing word from the final item:

▶ 11 = peoplc (F)

▶ 14 = savage (F)

▶ 18 = worshipping figure (O)

▶ 27 = stupid (D)

▶ 29 = keeping guard (W)

▶ 38 = rope (C)

▶ 39 = haggle (B)

▶ 41 and 43 = stream (G)

▶ 45 = _____ (F)

(13) THEMED PAIRS

Form four common pairs from the following group of items:

▶ De-creasing

▶ Firedog

▶ Flower with yellow or orange heads

▶ Glittering paper

▶ Implore

▶ 18th century Irish dramatist

▶ Swift-flying songbird

▶ Starring

14 MUSICAL WORDS

Each of these phrases suggests a seven-letter word, with those words arranged in alphabetical order. Can you identify the musical feature they have in common?

▶ Came to the throne

▶ Emotional problems

▶ Round vegetable

▶ Spoiled by overwriting

▶ Removed to render invisible

▶ Main front of a building

▶ Choked

15 A BIT TO EAT

Six teenagers went for a meal at the A1 Cafe. They soon realized, however, that one item was missing from the menu. Can you figure out what it was, too?

Here's what they ate:

	Apple pie	Ice cream	Burger	Fries	Drink
Anne		✓			
Barney		✓	✓	✓	✓
Coleen	✓		✓		
David			✓		
Erica		✓	✓	✓	✓
Frank			✓	✓	✓

(16) VENN 3

Can you identify the rules used to sort the elements in this Venn diagram?

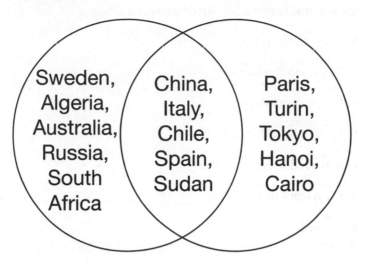

(17) EXTRA

Can you spot the common feature of the following terms?

▶ Source of ready cash

▶ Flat-panel optical device

▶ Cold War disarmament mechanism

▶ Retrovirus that was first clinically observed in 1981

▶ Means of accessing a bank machine

(18) IT'S ALL GREEK TO ME

The following table consists of twelve items that are to be divided into four groups of three. A common addition to each group of three is to be deduced. Definitions of each item with the common element included are given first:

▶ Computing connection

▶ Disaster

▶ Exaggeration

▶ One way to leave an aircraft

▶ Possible scenario

▶ Spanish hotel

▶ Suffering an abnormality of movement and behaviour

▶ Superstore

▶ Tissue type

▶ Type of syringe

▶ Underground burial site

▶ Wall

The words in the table are as follows:

Link	Chute	Market
Comb	Pet	Tonic
Dor	Strophe	Blast
Dermic	Thesis	Bole

(19) AUTHORITATIVE COMMENTS

Can you identify the common source of comments contained in the following pieces of text, all of which have been treated in the same way?

▶ RDMY LPSN NWT XS

▶ THNL YTHN GWHV TFRS FRTS LF

▶ MYFL LWMRC NSSK NTWH TYRC NTRYC NDFR YSKW HTYC NDFRY RCNTRY

▶ NVRT RSTM NNLS SVGT HSPC KRNM YPCKT

▶ FYWN TFRN DNW SHNG TNG TDG

▶ BLSS DRTH YNGFR THYSHL LNHRT THNT NLDBT

▶ YMYF LLLT HPPL SMF THTM YCNV NFLS MFTH PPLL LTHT MBT YCN TFL LLFT HPPL LLTHTM

(20) CLIMBER'S DIVISION

Can you identify eight members of a noted group suggested by the following hints (both cryptic and straight), finding the missing member?

▶ UK prime minister

▶ South American country broadcast

▶ Former US grunge musician

▶ British naval college

▶ Dutch territory?

▶ Singer with weight

▶ Key supplier

(21) PERIODIC PAIRS

Can you split the following items into pairs by applying them to different members of a noted group? Some items could suit several members, were it not necessary to form them into pairs.

Ash	Black
Bloody	Casual
Cyber	Good
Holy	Lazarus
Maundy	Palm
Plough	Shrove
Spy	Super

(22) BACK TO THE BEGINNING?

The following is a table of contents illustrating a set of items. Can you identify the other letter that has to accompany E as corresponding to 10?

▶ 4: B × 2 , F, P, T

▶ 5: A × 2 , G, H, N, O, T × 2

▶ 6: A, C, H, M, P, R, T × 2, W

▶ 7: C, H, J × 3, K, L, M

▶ 8: B, C, F, G, H × 2, M, V

▶ 9: C, J, R × 2

▶ 10: E, _____

(23) LEADERS OF THE GODS

The numbers below represent translations of the names of the Olympian gods. Can you complete the missing number?

▶ Zeus = -16

▶ Hera = +2

▶ Poseidon = -2

▶ Demeter = -1

▶ Athena = +12

▶ Apollo = +0

▶ Artemis = +3

▶ Ares = +12

▶ Aphrodite = +21

▶ Hephaestus = +14

▶ Hermes = +5

▶ Hestia = +14

▶ Dionysus = _____

(24) BILINGUAL GIBBERISH

The following phrases express the same sentiment in four different languages. Can you identify the key phrase, hinted at by the title, that would be used in English?

▶ Parang intsik

▶ Questo per me è arabo

▶ Gi estas Volapuko por mi

▶ C'est du chinois

25 PUNAGRAMS 5

Solve the anagrams below to reveal eight sports. However, each anagram has one letter missing. In order, these missing letters read to give an answer to this question:

What sport do Phoebe, Monica, Rachel, Chandler and Joey play? (4,4)

▶ FOG   _____   _

▶ CHERRY   _____   _

▶ SCORE   _____   _

▶ TALL BABES   _____   _

▶ OK NOSE   _____   _

▶ SUM   _____   _

▶ NEWT GIRL   _____   _

▶ QUASH   _____   _

26 KLUMP 2

Shade some circles so that the remaining numbers are joined together into groups of one, two or three circles. The sum of the numbers in each group must match one of the totals provided. Each total is used exactly once. Groups may not touch each other, and neither may shaded circles.

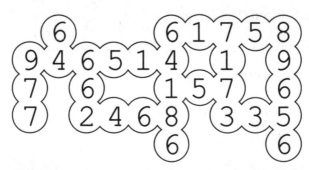

Totals: 5   7   8   10   11   13   14   20   22

(27) MISSION ACTIVITY

Each word in the following list has a common property to be found. The leftovers can then be arranged to denote something that might be used to describe their activity.

▶ Pliant

▶ Krona

▶ Lemon

▶ Negate

▶ Peerless

▶ Putto

▶ Reforming

▶ Sedate

▶ Unbelt

(28) STAGE

Can you identify the common connection between the following?

▶ Lawrence (Hamlet)

▶ Russell (As You Like It)

▶ Richardson (The Tempest)

▶ Bell (Macbeth)

▶ Banderas (The Merchant of Venice)

▶ Winslet (The Taming of the Shrew)

(29) NUMBER SEQUENCE

What number and city would be next in the following
sequence?

▶ 2 = Sydney

▶ 6 = Athens

▶ 10 = Beijing

▶ 5 = London

(30) TABLE OF CITIES

Which city could follow next in this list?

▶ Galway (31)

▶ Geneva (32)

▶ Asmara (33)

▶ Seattle (34)

(31) PERSONAL CONNECTION

Can you identify the factor that links each of the following?

▶ King John

▶ James II

▶ William IV

▶ Raúl Castro

(32) LANGUAGE TOUR

Can you identify which places would be being referred to in the following list, if you were in each given country at the time?

▶ Mailand (Germany)

▶ Monaco (Italy)

▶ Aix-la-Chapelle (France)

▶ Rijsel (Holland)

▶ Wien (Germany)

▶ Bryste (Wales)

▶ Ginebra (Spain)

▶ Pressburg (Germany)

(33) BOARD

Six single words and one two-word term have a common property, and their outstanding feature could form something that is commonly associated with them. What is that thing?

▶ Crude

▶ Facet

▶ Tribe

▶ Amend

▶ Abound

▶ Snottily

▶ Poor niche

(34) MIDDLESIX 2

Arrange the letters of the word CAFETERIA into the empty grid squares to create six five-letter words, three reading across and three reading down.

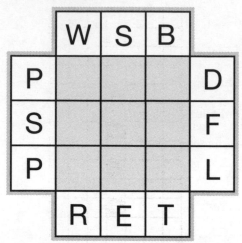

(35) SEQUENCE 2

In this sequence, what item might come next?

► Ocean

► Constitution

► Empire

► Garden

► First

► Old Line

► Old Dominion

► Tar Heel

► Palmetto

► Peach

(36) ALAN'S CURIOUS QUEST

Follow the clues chronologically to locate a Narnian treasure on the map below.

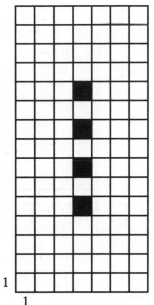

1

1

▶ Lucy Looks into a Wardrobe / How Shasta Set Out on His Travels / The Island / The Picture in the Bedroom / Behind the Gym/ Jill is Given a Task / The Sailing of the King

▶ Back on This Side of the Door / Prince Corin / The Storm and What Came of It / Puddleglum/

▶ A Day with the Beavers / Aravis in Tashbaan / How the Adventure Ended/ The Hill of the Strange Trenches / The House of Harfang / How They Discovered Something Worth Knowing / The Island of the Voices / Across the Desert / In the Witch's House / What Happened After Dinner

▶ In the Dark Castle / The Dufflepuds Made Happy / The Unwelcome Fellow Traveller / Aslan is Nearer / Peter's First Battle / Deep Magic from the Dawn of Time / The Fight at Anvard / The High King in Command / The Three Sleepers / Underland Without the Queen

▶ The Disappearance of Jill

(37) FANDE

What elementary link connects the following characters?

▶ Gehrig (horse)

▶ Van Gaal (tulip)

▶ Wellington (duke)

▶ Bismarck (chancellor)

(38) SEQUENCE 3

What sequence is demonstrated by the following literary passages, and what title might one expect to find at the end of the series outlined below?

▶ 'Some of the evil of my tale may have been inherent in the circumstances. For years we lived anyhow with one another in the naked desert, under the indifferent heaven.'

▶ 'I can't see. Let's have a little light please.'

▶ 'All this happened, more or less.'

▶ 'Sherlock Holmes took his bottle from the corner of the mantelpiece and his hypodermic syringe from its neat morocco case.'

▶ 'There were four of us – George, and William Samuel Harris, and myself, and Montmerency.'

▶ 'It was the best of times, it was the worst of times, it was the age of wisdom, it was the age of foolishness.'

▶ 'At five o'clock that morning, reveille was sounded as usual by the blow of a hammer on a length of rail hanging up near the staff quarters.'

(39) EVEN MORE TANGLED DUOS

Untangle each pair of related words. The letters in each pair are in the correct order for each component word, but the components can be mixed in any way.

For example, WBLHACITKE = BLACK and WHITE

► YAYNING

► HALARURDELY

► BIPITESCES

► SEVERENANUAS

► WILKLAIATME

► THEAADILSS

► SLANDADERKESS

► PINNEEDLESS

► SCARTIROCKT

► VECHARPTERSE

► MOPERSTARTLE

► FAFUSRIOTUS

► HASMICKMERLE

► LOPROSFITS

► ALOMPEGAHA

(40) GO WITH THE FLOW

What would come next in the following sequence of related items?

▶ Baht

▶ Riel

▶ Dong

(41) TRANSFORMATION

What historical connection links the following?

▶ Betjeman

▶ Alsatian

▶ Hot dog

▶ Liberty cabbage

▶ Windsor

(42) TYPES

What particular feature do the following all have in common?

▶ Prince

▶ Oslo

▶ Leyton Orient

▶ Gmail

▶ Cape Canaveral

(43) MINI BARRED CROSSWORD

Solve the clues, and place the entries in the crossword grid according to the clue numbers. Bars indicate the ends of entries.

```
+----+----+----+----+
| 1  | 2  | 3  | 4  |
+----+----+----+----+
|    | 5  |    |    |
+----+----+----+----+
| 6  | 7  | 8  | 9  |
+----+----+----+----+
|    | 10 |    |    |
+----+----+----+----+
```

Across

1. English county (2)
3. Consequences (2)
5. French woman (2)
6. Card game (2)
8. Pascoe's partner (2)
10. Adversary (3)

Down

1. Composition (2)
2. Do well (2)
3. Turkish Mr (3)
4. Too much (2)
6. Like some whiskies (2)
7. Pepper (2)
9. Goulding (2)

(44) EXCHANGE

What links the following items, and can you identify a related word that is created as the link is deduced?

▶ Drain

▶ Fuel

▶ Innard

▶ Love

▶ Prose

▶ Route

(45) STATE YOUR NAME

How should the following first names and surnames be paired? There will be one first name left over, for which you should invent an appropriate surname to pair it with.

FIRST NAMES	SURNAMES
Alan	Attlee
Blaise	Harrison
Connor	Landor
Deirdre	Lassiter
Dietrich	Leighton
Dora	Mondrian
Klaus	Parker
Ogden	Ronson
Paloma	Singleton
Tristam	Tindall
Vidal	Vernon
Zak	_____

(46) A LAKE IN A COUNTRY?

Which member of a group of six is missing in the following list?

▶ All directions bar east

▶ Question lethal dosage

▶ Salvation Army

▶ Teaching assistant society

▶ Six hundred

(47) ISOLATE I

Draw walls to partition the grid into six areas, such that each area contains two stars. The six areas must each have one of the sizes shown beneath the grid, in terms of the number of squares that make up that area. Each '+' must be linked to at least two walls, and each listed area size must be used exactly once.

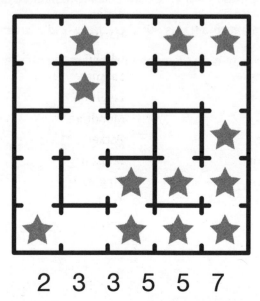

2 3 3 5 5 7

(48) TV PUZZLE

The local television station is preparing its nightly news cast, which contains four 'feel good' segments. Use the clues to determine which segment airs during which time slot, who is reporting each segment, and how long each segment runs for.

▶ Olivia's segment ran before the segment about a surgical breakthrough, but after the two-minute segment

▶ The longest segment was either about the world's largest cat or was the segment in which Nancy reported

▶ Neither of the two longest segments aired last

▶ Pete's segment, which was longer than Martin's, was about either an art gallery opening or seasonal produce

▶ The segment about the art gallery opening was two minutes shorter than the one about seasonal produce

▶ The shortest segment was aired before the produce segment

▶ Neither Nancy nor Pete had their segment aired first

▶ Martin's segment was not about the world's largest cat

▶ The four-minute segment aired before the cat segment

	2 Minutes	3 Minutes	4 Minutes	5 Minutes	Art Gallery	Large Cat	Produce	Surgery	Martin	Nancy	Olivia	Pete
7:00 PM												
7:15 PM												
7:30 PM												
7:45 PM												
Martin												
Nancy												
Olivia												
Pete												
Art Gallery												
Large Cat												
Produce												
Surgery												

(49) TWO'S COMPANY I

Which of the following words is the odd one out?

RAIN	DRAGON
COW	RADISH
GROUND	HORSE
WHERE	DOWN
NIGHT	BOW
POUR	EARTH
FLY	DOG
ANY	CUP
BULL	HOG
CODE	MARE
BUTTER	BAR
JACK	POT
BOY	

(50) FEATURE 5

Can you identify the common feature of the following words?

▶ Choir

▶ Rhythm

▶ Ghoul

▶ Echo

▶ Aghast

▶ Rhinoceros

(51) CONNECTION CLICHÉ

Can you identify the common link in the following?

▶ A woman who is unconventionally beautiful

▶ Disorientation in a foreign environment

▶ Aimless urban stroller

▶ Something discovered by chance

▶ Staircase wit

(52) FEATURE 6

Can you identify the common feature of the following words?

▶ Two

▶ Whole

▶ Sword

▶ Answer

Chapter 4
Encrypted

Turing made many breakthroughs
during his work on codebreaking
at Bletchley Park in the 1940s.
Some of his methods were so
important that they were only
declassified as recently as
2012, remaining useful and
relevant for 70 years — a
remarkable amount of time, when
you consider the advances in
computing that have taken place
since then. See if you too can
crack some thornier problems
in this next chapter — which
includes some encrypted text.

ⓘ BLETCHLEY PARK CROSSWORD

Bletchley Park once used a cryptic crossword to find recruits for its early code-cracking efforts. Try solving *this* themed cryptic puzzle, noting that perimeter letters are significant.

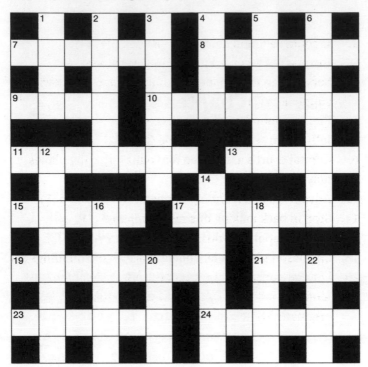

ACROSS

7. Making inquiry in a ruling capacity? (6)
8. Personal declaration by ex-PM, we hear, forming part for viewer (3-3)
9. Very little military intelligence on province (4)
10. Learner suffering to lose strength (8)
11. Computers etc staged for analysis following essence of logic (7)
13. Hotel by a top Asian capital (5)
15. Decorators – leaderless people taking risks? (5)
17. Allows modern technology in waves (7)
19. Inactive before start of decryption regarding some codes? (8)

21. University lecturer first with note in game (4)
23. Those ending intelligence mission connect order (6)
24. Side with number of characters in cryptograph? (6)

DOWN
1. It could be found among Verona's tipple? (4)
2. Income not recorded mostly in government (6)
3. Serviceman fired among outsiders in agency showing suppleness (7)
4. Element found in machine once (4)
5. Jellyfish in sea by home of the CIA (6)
6. Capital court's assembled for youth following planes, maybe (3, 5)
12. Advantage in a manning of operations, it's said (8)
14. Stop in back making one more prepared (7)
16. Fine material in bands for part of typewriter (6)
18. Spymaster given independent place as surroundings (6)
20. Foreign queen in country after leader's demoted (4)
22. Limited intake that is filling decoding team originally (4)

② COMMON FEATURES 5

What is the common feature of all of these words and phrases?

▶ Location

▶ Untied

▶ Piano repairer

▶ Pampering

③ TIKTAKA I

This puzzle consists of two grids constructed using the same set of shapes. A path must be drawn through each grid so that each bold-lined shape is visited exactly once. The ends of the path and some of the inner route are shown. Wherever the path passes through identical shapes in each grid, the route of the path must be exactly the same, although it may be rotated and/or reflected relative to the other grid.

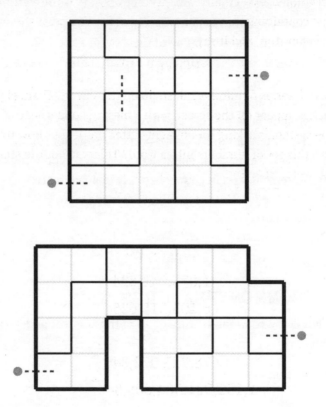

④ WELCOME TO PUZZLANDIA

The following six puzzles are related, and lead to an overall meta puzzle which requires you to have solved the first five first.

— — —

The *Puzzlandia* Puzzle Championships are just around the corner! You've applied and have been eagerly awaiting your ticket for weeks. Finally, an envelope appears through the post containing, to your surprise, a tablet. You press the power button, and it says:

POWER UP

Next, a series of numbers flash up on the screen. Then, eight dashes appear on the screen with a message underneath. The system is asking for an eight-letter word – but how to turn this set of numbers into a word? This was not the start you were expecting.

1

16,777,216

43,046,721

1,073,741,824

6,103,515,625

7,776

678,223,072,849

1,152,921,504,606,846,976

USE YOUR POWERS TO ENTER THE PASSWORD:

— — — — — — — —

⑤ *** OFF!

This puzzle continues a story from the previous puzzle.

You enter the password and breathe a sigh of relief. 'Congratulations,' it says, 'Your place in the Puzzlandia Puzzle Championships has been reserved. We'll see you there. In the mean time, do you like contests? Then you'll love these!'

Morse contest?	? _ _ _	Leave quickly
Beauty contest?	_ _ _ ?	Start an ice hockey game
Jazz's Davis's contest?	? _ _ _ _	Nowhere near
Agreement contest?	_ ? _	Go to sleep
Rambling contest?	_ _ ? _	Get rid of stiffness
Political-slanting contest?	_ _ ? _	CSI: Miami or Torchwood
Pedestal contest?	_ ? _ _ _	Impasse
Mining contest?	_ ? _ _	Bring down one by one
Diving contest?	_ _ ? _	Deliver
Bed-building contest?	_ _ ? _	Shirk from work
Timekeeping contest?	? _ _ _ _	Stop working
Lumberjacking contest?	_ ? _	Stop working on a computer
Applause contest?	_ _ ? _	Transfer to another person
Actors' contest?	_ _ _ ?	Remove rope from mooring
Mozzarella-eating contest?	_ _ _ ? _ _	Annoy
Theatrical contest?	? _ _ _	Swagger
Election contest?	_ _ ? _	Eliminate, as on Survivor
Shouting contest?	_ _ _ ?	Cancel
Relaxing contest?	_ ? _	Fire
Aerial crop-feeding contest?	_ ? _ _	Clean after a period without use

CD-making contest?   _ _ _ ?   Use up energy

Insect contest?   _ _ ? _   Complete, as a list

Wrestling contest?   ? _ _ _   Wait

⑥ FEEL LIKE A MEGA HERO

This puzzle continues a story from the previous two puzzles.

The contests disappear from the tablet, to be replaced with lots of circles. It *feels* important.

○○ ○○ ○○ ₄	○○ ○○ ○○ ₃	○○ ○○ ○○ ₃	○○ ○○ ○○ ₂	②② ③③ ①①
○○ ○○ ○○ ₃	○○ ○○ ○○ ₃	○○ ○○ ○○ ₁	○○ ○○ ○○ ₄	②③ ②① ③⓪
○○ ○○ ○○ ₄	○○ ○○ ○○ ₃	○○ ○○ ○○ ₃	○○ ○○ ○○ ₄	③② ②② ④①
○○ ○○ ○○ ₃	○○ ○○ ○○ ₃	○○ ○○ ○○ ₂	○○ ○○ ○○ ₂	④② ⓪② ②⓪
①④ ③③ ②①	④② ①② ③⓪	④① ⓪① ②①	②② ③② ③⓪	

⑦ ON THE WAY

This puzzle continues a story from the previous three puzzles.

Looking back at the tablet, the location of the Puzzlandia Puzzle Championships has been revealed. The following message then appears: 'Before the event, you should solve this puzzle. It will tell you how to get to the Championships, and what you should do beforehand.' So you attempt to solve the puzzle:

⑧ PASSWORD

This puzzle continues a story from the previous four
puzzles.

You arrive at the Puzzlandia Puzzle Championships. The
doors remain closed and there's a guard outside. He gives
you this riddle:

Forgotten the password?

Let me fill you with dread.

I made up this ditty,

So others are deterred,

In a *poetic scheme*.

I'm a literature nerd!

But when parsing it all,

For the line that is third,

Use R instead,

Then go back to C.

What is it you have inferred?

Forgotten the password? You were never given the
password! But now you realize what you have to do...

⑨ WHAT'S THE META?

This puzzle continues a story from the previous five puzzles, which you will need to have solved in order to solve this one.

You finally get in and you can see the Puzzle Championships on the other side of the hall, but there's a grid of letters on the floor between you and the exit. Thinking about all the tasks set to you so far, you navigate through it and give the bouncer waiting at the exit one more word. What is that word?

EXIT

	L	O	R		A
O		B	K		A
	T	T	A	D	A
H		E	A		C
P	A		R	T	
L		H	B		A
I	T				N
V	Y	R	O	I	
E	U	H	A		A
D				V	E
E	R	A	D		T
	N	T		B	
E		A	T		L
N	O			K	
	E	P		N	
E	X		S		A

ENTER

(10) NEXT IN LINE 2

What should come next in each of the following real-world sequences, and why?

▶ O   T   T   F   F   S

▶ V   I   B   G   Y   O

▶ M   N   B   V   C   X

▶ H   H   L   B   B   C

▶ C   G   D   A   E   B

(11) KEYWORDS

Thanks to recent developments, such occurrences are now fortunately rather rare – but under what circumstances might a barmaid be seen to create carnage, with Smirnoff being poisoned and a pint likely to get you shot?

(12) MIXING PAINT

The three 'rails' on a fence need painting, but which three paints should be used?

P L A T W U P E C R E B O N R S L R

(13) STILL ON THE ROAD

In Serbia you came across a large bed, whereas in Algeria you saw a sea girl, and in Australia a care barn. What did you receive in Peru?

(14) MINI 5×5 JIGSAW

Solve the clues, which are arranged alphabetically in order of their full solution. Enter them where they fit, so as to fill the crossword grid. Bars indicate the ends of entries.

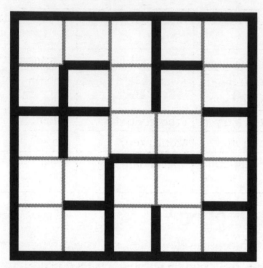

Is there a problem? (4)

Disagree (2)

Bohemian (2)

Intense watch (3)

Netanyahu (2)

Sweetheart (2)

Secretive (2)

Tropical resin (3)

Cockney greeting (2)

Void (2)

Power (3)

Jealousy (2)

Here in France (2)

You've done me a favour (3)

Understand (2)

Spanish relative (2)

Monkey (2)

Palish (2)

(15) TWO BOYS

Five members of a historical group are to be identified in the table below. Reading across the table, each relates in the same way to the different members of the group.

ECHO GROUP	BREAKDOWN GROUP	TYPE GROUP
Tree pitch	As a hotel	Montana
Northern Ireland town sea fog	Award a hectare	Lincoln
Converted a try	Proceed lord	Palladium
Alaskan capital	Month zero	Diana
Flock of mallards	Special language unit	Spear

(16) GC&CS KEYWORD CYPHER

In terms of UK intelligence, if ORHRECVJ VKPORFOGJVT was GYGH JKFCHM in JTR CPCJGJCSH MGPR depicting events at OYRJVTYRX LGFA, can you determine what code is being used and the name of the place that forms its basis?

(17) WAVE DOWN

Here's the ripest mix-up. For each line, flag up what is happening and calculate the missing answer. If you get cross, that may be a sign.

- ▶ Netherlands, Scotland, Ukraine   = 6

- ▶ Thailand, Switzerland, Russia   = 8

- ▶ USA, Jamaica, Japan   = 0

- ▶ Germany, England, Argentina   = _____

(18) OPERATIONS

Solve the cryptic clues below and write the answers in the grid, which will then give you a thirteenth one in the central column. The clues also provide openings to an additional hint as to the identity of the thirteenth item, barring an indefinite article.

1. Bungling aim with confused males surrounding church festival (10)
2. Rockfall in this area, northern Switzerland, in a depressed feature (9)
3. In charge of peer and superior (8)
4. Device in winery, perhaps, with Irish port's staff (9)
5. Grub nice team cooked after mass (9)
6. Especially prickly plant caught in California by American (6)
7. Troubling changes, not for all to see in fastener (8)
8. Ox-like creature in New York city (7)
9. One that could be called upon for engagement? (9)
10. Fall behind rate unusually – an emotional sign (8)
11. Awkwardly move sailor, worker in timber (10)
12. Rollicking grandee making explosive device (7)

(19) STACKED TIPS

Can you identify the common property of the words with
the given meanings in the following stack? The words are of
increasing length in the stack, and the clue to each word is
a definition of the full word plus a cryptic indication of the
remainder of the word that *excludes* the common property.

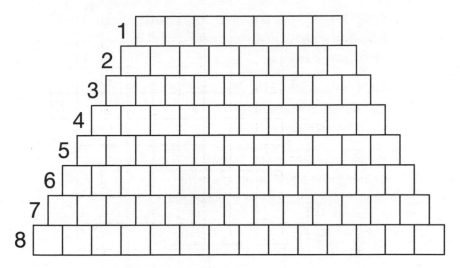

1. Expert soprano
2. Irrational number breathes
3. One badgering servants?
4. Style of music by Frenchman in a luring process?
5. Return of horrible figure around river in secret
6. Gas or liquid containing iodine in description of natural
   phenomena
7. Diversion in a term that's altered
8. Sprayer, say, one for each gentleman containing
   phosphorus

⟨20⟩ WORD SQUARE

The answers to each of the three parts of this question
consist of three letters. When you have solved each part,
write the answers in order from top to bottom in the 3×3
grid. The name of a person is then traceable in the grid,
although letters may be visited more than once.

▶ What three-letter acronym can be inserted into all of the
  following words to make four new words?
  Coder, pet, seat, sting

▶ What real word could be consistent in meaning with the
  following unreal words?
  Etalp, latem, nac, yenom

▶ Which set of letters starts words with the following
  meanings in ascending order of size?
  Food, rough, US rock music, complaint

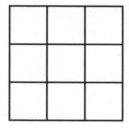

⟨21⟩ FIESTA OF FUN

Can you identify the common link between the following?

▶ Conversation at a table after the end of a meal

▶ A relationship between in-laws

▶ A person who is blind in one eye

▶ Sense of awe and inspiration from nature

▶ To go out and eat a snack

(22) TRANSFORMATIONS

Match up the five final clues to their other halves.

PALE	♣	Bucket
	♦	Jump *or* Bell sound
	♥	Friend
	♠	Force 8 wind *or* Story

DAMP ♥ ♠ ♦ ♠ ♣ _____

EARTH ♦ ♥ ♠ ♦ ♥ _____

STUDY ♦ ♥ ♠ ♥ ♦ _____

STAGE ♦ ♥ ♣ ♠ ♣ _____

YEARLY ♠ ♥ ♥ ♣ ♠ _____

▶ Hawaiian garment

▶ Head covering

▶ Heaviness

▶ Sandwich

▶ Scrap of cloth

(23) NUMBER TRICK

The number 1,709,835,264 contains every digit from zero to nine once each.

▶ Multiply this number by 2. What do you notice?

▶ Now multiply the original number by 5. What *two* things do you notice?

(24) SALVATION ARMY RANKS

Can you match the items in the following four lists to put
them into linked groups of four, with one from each list in
every set? All items are used.

LIST A

▶ Assumption

▶ Enclosure outside of the field

▶ Middle of the world

▶ Good airs

▶ Saint James

▶ I saw a mount

▶ Talker

▶ The peace

LIST B

▶ A cousin

▶ Mail

▶ Noted movie

▶ Oat gains

▶ Plaza

▶ Quoit

▶ Serious bean

▶ Tobago

LIST C

▶ Rear Admiral

▶ Best of luck

▶ Easily completed

▶ Caught off-guard

▶ Physical education

▶ Pretty youth

▶ Residential care home

▶ Ultimately yours

LIST D

▶ SLMHFPRFS

▶ UERBH

▶ OGBRVRS

▶ UGBGDORS

▶ JSLSMQSY

▶ HUQSTGL

▶ JHLQ

▶ QLQMQSY

(25) HAIL!

MXYSX SQUIQH HKBUT YD JXU OUQH (QT)
UGKQB JE JXU IXYVJ KIUT YD JXYI CUIIQWU?

26 VENN 4

Can you identify the rule used to sort the elements in this
Venn diagram?

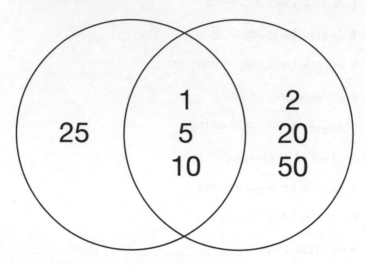

27 FLAG TIME

What type of flag do the following times represent?

▶ 10:00

▶ 3:45

▶ 7:50

▶ 6:50

▶ 9:55

▶ 1:40

▶ 9:50

▶ 10:10

▶ 9:15

(28) FIRST REVISIONS

Can you work out what I was doing at 11pm?

▶ At 2am, I was conveying

▶ At 6am, I was worrying

▶ At 7am, I was putting on a harness

▶ At 8am, I was listening

▶ At 2pm, I was approaching

▶ At 6pm I was raising

▶ At 7pm, I was cauterizing

▶ At 8pm, I was ripping

▶ At 11pm, I was _____

(29) THE LONG AND SHORT OF IT

What am I doing here?

Taking each word,

And hearing

How it sounds.

One for dit. Two

For dah.

Keeping fit

Running. Handsome Morse?

(30) SUFFIX TO SAY

With an L or an S, I'm a giver upon request,

With G I'm a woman, man or whatever describes best,

With an F and then a B, I'm an accident with blame,

But tell me, with nothing else, who wrote my game?

(31) TANGLED TRIOS

Untangle each triplet of related words. The letters in each puzzle are in the correct order for each component word, but the components can be mixed in any way.

For example, SILGOBVLERRONZED = GOLD, SILVER and BRONZE

▶ PROLONGSPLIVERE

▶ THRONETWEEO

▶ LOBSTARRECLOCKK

▶ HARDTRICKYOM

▶ WARWILDROTICOBHEN

▶ CARDPAROVERMINAROGOATTSI

▶ APARTOARHOTMISSHOS

▶ SCRAPNOCKPLEAP

▶ BRAMAROURBRINICEY

 32 FOUR BY FOUR 3

Solve the clues and fit their answers into the 4×4 grid, so they read either across or down. Each answer is four letters long. To make things trickier, the clues are given in no particular order. One letter is already filled in.

▶ Keep out of sight

▶ Routes

▶ Eastern European capital

▶ Food

▶ Leer

▶ Social insects

▶ In a carefree manner

▶ Child's bed

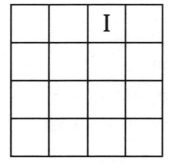

(33) NO MAN'S LAND

I have some strange codes in my passport. Where have I been?

- ▶ FVGLZ KPWQS NYJRT ADBUH

- ▶ GWTPF LJVEX KYIQB MZC

- ▶ JSOQP TIYUZ GXWFH BLVC

- ▶ LJWDY CRPGQ HXVOF M

- ▶ YGOPM JFUXH QVCKB

- ▶ IDOFS WKBLZ XECMQ JPTV

- ▶ WMSOD IQVXJ TBUYL GKPZH

- ▶ HRWPZ XQKJF BUDYT MGC

- ▶ CUGQF JKWPR HZSDY XLOB

- ▶ JFVXN CQZIK YGOPT DWHM

(34) MIDDLESIX 3

Arrange the letters of the word CALCULATE into the empty grid squares to create six five-letter words, three reading across and three reading down.

	S	M	E	
S				K
J				Y
M				W
	K	H	T	

(35) ANYTHING ELSE?

Can you associate each of the clues with the words in this list, and then use the result of this association to reveal an appropriate phrase?

GRIN	SPAR
PIT	CARED
SEVER	EAT
LIP	PANT
CURT	PRICE
TEE	ROUND

- ▶ 568ml
- ▶ Sea barrier, in the US
- ▶ Carried
- ▶ Decorate a wall
- ▶ Extra
- ▶ Walk with difficulty
- ▶ Harsh
- ▶ Increase in temperature
- ▶ Large wooden plant
- ▶ Monarch's son
- ▶ Soil
- ▶ Woo

(36) CRYPTIC MOVIE CLUB I

The schedule for our Movie Club this season has been devised by a crossword setter, who has imagined each movie title to be a cryptic clue with a one-word solution. For example, OBSESS = Horrible Bosses (anagram – 'horrible' – of BOSSES), CHILL = Cold Mountain (C+HILL), and POM = Love In The Afternoon (O in PM). From the following list of 'solutions', can you identify the original titles? The length of each word in the original movie title is given.

▶ REASON (5,1,3)

▶ A-LEVEL (3,5,3)

▶ PASTA (4,4)

▶ HECTARE (3,7)

▶ ADAGES (6,5)

▶ WINO (5,2,4)

▶ INSOLE (4,5)

(37) ODD CLUE OUT

Which of the following is the odd one out?

▶ The Big Sleep, for example

▶ State-appointed attorney, in the US

▶ Three Erik Satie compositions

▶ Women's tennis team competition

▶ Theatrical stand-in

(38) MORTPANTEAUX

How should these words be more properly spelled?

▶ PARIONETTE: _ _ _ _ _ _ _

▶ ROLETUME: _ _ _ _ _ _ _ _

▶ HOMBAY: _ _ _ _ _ _ _ _ _ _

▶ FOON: _ _ _ _ _

▶ POMERINE: _ _ _ _ _ _ _ _

▶ LEAKFAST: _ _ _ _ _ _ _

▶ FOKE: _ _ _ _

▶ CAMFORD: _ _ _ _ _ _ _ _ _

▶ EGANTIC: _ _ _ _ _ _ _ _ _ _

▶ BIDEO: _ _ _ _

(39) STEP-BY-STEP

If you solve this puzzle in a step-by-step way, you will end up with one, appropriate, word. What is that word?

▶ 4922945 1452420 12914519 225 2081855

▶ 55567554585 4357260 38743557

▶ 124506 33936 1625763 727623 243574539

▶ 11740584486756963435396 1173 755202633 155442

(40) POKER PUZZLE

Your opponent holds a five-card poker hand with all the cards having face values of 10, Jack, Queen, King or Ace.

You have five guesses to identify all of their cards:

▶ To the left of each guess, a white dot indicates a card of the right suit in the wrong place, while a black dot means a card of the right suit is in the right place

▶ To the right of each guess, a white dot indicates a card of the right value in the wrong place, while a black dot means a card of the right value is in the right place

What hand do they hold?

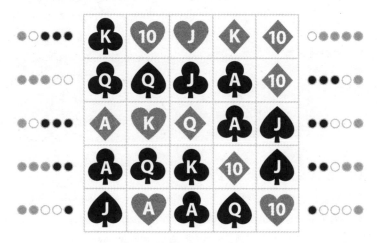

(41) APT PROPERTY I

In the word AMBIDEXTROUS, how might the left-hand and right-hand sides be considered well-matched?

Chapter 5
Enigmatic

Cracking the enciphered text produced by the Enigma machine was the ultimate test for Alan Turing and his colleagues at Bletchley Park. Now it's time for your own ultimate test — can you crack the hardest puzzles this book has to offer?

(1) ODD PAIR OUT I

The following twelve words can be joined into six pairs.
Which is the odd pair out?

▸ Adult

▸ Antic

▸ Bouts

▸ Clone

▸ Deter

▸ Lines

▸ Orate

▸ Paste

▸ Rated

▸ Riser

▸ There

▸ Tramp

(2) TWO'S COMPANY 2

What comes next in each of the following real-world
sequences, and why?

▸	_NE*	_WO*	_HR*	_OU*	_IV*	_IX*
▸	*ED	*GE	*OW	*EN	*UE	*GO
▸	WH*	HA*	TH*	QU*	FI*	SI*
▸	KI*	PH*	CL*	OR*	FA*	GE*
▸	F*T	S*D	T*D	F*H	F*H	S*H

③ FLOWERS OF THE UK

Which of these could produce a flower from France?

► Alfalfa

► Sycamore

► Laurel

► Vervain

► Muskroot

► Lousewort

④ GRIDFILL I

Fill the grid below with letters, one to each square, in such a way that each one of the seven colours of the rainbow – RED, ORANGE, YELLOW, GREEN, BLUE, INDIGO and VIOLET – can be traced by starting at a letter and moving through adjacent squares horizontally and vertically, but not diagonally. Double letters must occupy two adjacent squares.

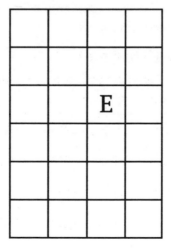

⑤ PROJECT RUNWAY

Air traffic control has a busy morning with multiple student pilots taking off in similar small craft at the local airport. Using both the clues and the runway map, match the student with their flight number, take-off runway assignment and order of departure.

▶ The craft piloted by Frank departed prior to the craft that took off from runway 36L

▶ The two aircraft with a nine in their flight numbers departed on parallel runways

▶ PUZ-4E2 departed on either runway 25L or 36L

▶ The third aircraft to depart, which was either PUZ-59D or PUZ-7CL, was not piloted by Greta

▶ The final departure was not a flight number ending with a letter

▶ Eli departed after the aircraft on runway 25L

▶ Dana piloted PUZ-59D

▶ Greta departed immediately prior to the aircraft on 36L

▶ The first two departures, neither of which were PUZ-9N3, departed on parallel runways

▶ PUZ-4E2 did not depart first

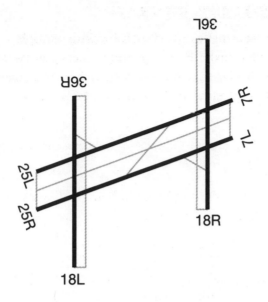

	Dana	Eli	Frank	Greta	PUZ-4E2	PUZ-59D	PUZ-7CL	PUZ-9N3	25L	25R	36L	36R
1st												
2nd												
3rd												
4th												
25L												
25R												
36L												
36R												
PUZ-4E2												
PUZ-59D												
PUZ-7CL												
PUZ-9N3												

⑥ TAKE A LETTER

Extract one letter from each of the following words, in a logical and consistent way, to form a seven-letter word. Using the same logic, which letter can then be extracted from this word?

▶ PILFER

▶ BLABBER

▶ NOMINATE

▶ ENQUIRED

▶ CLATTER

▶ TRIFLE

▶ BASTE

⑦ WORD MAESTRO

Can you identify the common language link in the following?

▶ Drowsiness from eating a big meal

▶ Lady who looks after stray cats

▶ To rest in the shade on a hot day

▶ A really badly made drink

⑧ POP SUMS I

If Smalltown Boy = More Than In Love, then solve (ignoring
definite articles):

▶ One Week = Make It With You + _____

▶ Viva La Vida + Big Log + The First Picture Of You
   = Pure Morning + Refugees + _____ + _____

⑨ RUN THE GAUNTLET

What is the common language link between the following?

▶ To be engaged in an activity that is comfortable or
   pleasurable

▶ A light mid-morning or mid-afternoon meal similar to
   afternoon tea

▶ To clear your throat

▶ Just the right amount

⑩ WORD BLUFF

Can you identify the common language link in the
following?

▶ Sitting back after a meal feeling full and satisfied

▶ Resting to allow an illness to take its course

▶ Going out in the wind to clear one's thoughts

▶ Cancelling plans by telephone

▶ Having a laissez-faire attitude to something

▶ Cosiness in a home environment

(11) OLD AND NEW

Can you join the following terms into pairs that fit together to make the clues to a particular set of words?

▶ Actual

▶ Aural

▶ Axe

▶ Broadsheet

▶ Cooker

▶ Cut

▶ Dawdler

▶ Match

▶ Morning

▶ Movie

▶ Post

▶ Presumptuous

▶ Racket sport

▶ Reserve

▶ Speechless

▶ Standard

▶ Transmit

▶ Unbending

(12) HUNT THE CHARACTER

Three components of a descriptive phrase are to be deduced in various ways. The phrase then has to be jumbled to form the name of a character.

The first component (2,8) has three different hints:

▶ The first is a standard cryptic clue: Supply free moralist as a prototype (8,4)

▶ The second can be defined as 'article' (2) followed by 'peculiarity' (6), creating a two-word term (2,6)

▶ The third could be depicted as: pe or imittion (3,1,4) – the method of describing either could be seen as a loose and somewhat whimsical definition of the component

The second component (5), which as a hint would be given as (4) in US English, has three exemplary cryptic clues each without a definition. Their common field forms the component. These are:

▶ Drink covering good cups? (8)

▶ Record freeze falling short (5)

▶ Hardened skin around much of incision (8)

The third component (3) has triple associations:

▶ The first is a word property demonstrated in a mixed-up, additive sense by the following: demon, taupe and notion

▶ The second is a word property that the following three words have in common: case, hatch, shell

▶ The third consists of synonyms that could be defined as polish (4) and cool (3)

The resulting phrase can be sifted to form a key character (4,8,6).

(13) VENN 5

Can you identify the rule used to sort the elements in this Venn diagram?

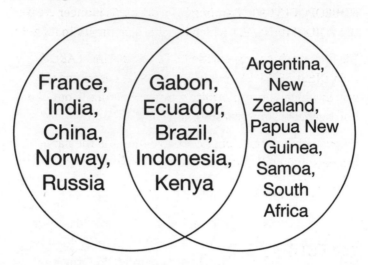

France, India, China, Norway, Russia

Gabon, Ecuador, Brazil, Indonesia, Kenya

Argentina, New Zealand, Papua New Guinea, Samoa, South Africa

(14) MIXED TRIAD

The following triad of words have a remarkable common feature that needs to be identified. Each word has a cryptic clue and there is an incidental hint of two letters in the clues when taken together in order.

▶ Altering sides, Thailand monarch is followed by donator, round figure in material with sheen

▶ A strap plus clothing and schedule with serviceman held back for person who studies matter again

▶ As an example, who and why is English Republican engaged in start before four in billionaire's keeping?

15 CODED TRIBUTE

Recognized as a HDQCMOCI HAPSTJ of AJPOHONOAG
OCPTGGOITCNT with creations such as the AQPDBAPON
NDBEQPOCI TCIOCT among his works, this pioneer created
the PQJOCI BANSOCT which became a landmark in its field.

His final research was entitled PST NSTBONAG LAKOK
DH BDJESDITCTKOK (published in 1952) describing the
way in which non-uniformity may arise naturally out of a
homogeneous, uniform state.

Can you deduce the cipher code to determine the name of
the person for whom this tribute is given?

16 ISOLATE 2

Draw walls to partition the grid into six areas, such that
each area contains two stars. The six areas must each have
one of the sizes shown beneath the grid, in terms of the
number of squares that make up that area. Each '+' must be
linked to at least two walls, and each listed area size must be
used exactly once.

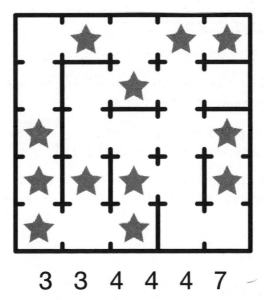

3   3   4   4   4   7

(17) CRYPTIC MOVIE CLUB 2

The schedule for our Movie Club this season has been devised by a crossword setter, who has imagined each movie title to be a cryptic clue with a one-word solution. For example, OBSESS = Horrible Bosses (anagram of BOSSES), CHILL = Cold Mountain (C+HILL), and POM = Love In The Afternoon (O in PM). From the following list of 'solutions', can you identify the original titles? The length of each word in the original movie title is given.

▶ AM (3,5,7)

▶ SCREWABLE (3,2,5)

▶ TAN (4,1,8)

▶ VINOUS (3,5,5)

▶ KEITH (4,4,2,3)

▶ EVOLVE (3,5,3)

▶ BIG (1,4,4,8)

(18) TITLE FEATURES

What common feature do the following movie titles all share? The years are provided as additional clues.

▶ Life of Brian (1968)

▶ Theatre of Blood (1995)

▶ The Krays (2004)

▶ A Clockwork Orange (1985)

▶ Brazil (1969)

▶ Babel (1995)

▶ Fargo (2012)

⑲ GRIDFILL 2

Fill the grid below with letters, one to each square, in such
a way that each one of the seven deadly sins – AVARICE,
ENVY, GLUTTONY, LUST, PRIDE, SLOTH and WRATH – can
be traced by starting at a letter and moving through adjacent
squares horizontally and vertically, but not diagonally.
What's more, the letters occupying the first and third rows
spell two words that have the same meaning, although the
first is archaic usage. What are those words? Double letters
must occupy two adjacent squares, and squares can be
revisited within a word.

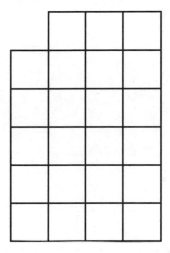

⑳ GLOBETROTTING 3

Which word is the 'longest'?

▶ MADDEN

▶ SEAMAN

▶ BOMBOS

▶ LAXIST

▶ HELLAS

21) EVEN MORE TANGLED TRIOS

Untangle each triplet of related words. The letters in each puzzle are in the correct order for each component word, but the components can be mixed in any way.

For example, SILGOBVLERRONZED = GOLD, SILVER and BRONZE

- ▶ CLAMOURRELYRY

- ▶ SHAMTIMERRRANUVIPL

- ▶ BLEATTCOMATOUTCONE

- ▶ LSMEARMADIGULLME

- ▶ FEARWITHINRED

- ▶ SHINLIKEROOKNE

- ▶ BAGDOUGLODY

- ▶ PALTUTORAMAINEOBINSLESS

- ▶ SLOGAILSQUIDID

22) VENN 6

Can you identify the rule used to sort the elements in this Venn diagram?

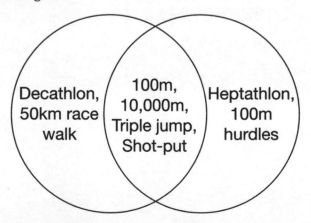

(23) TIKTAKA 2

This puzzle consists of two grids constructed using the same set of shapes. A path must be drawn through each grid so that each bold-lined shape is visited exactly once. The ends of the path and some of the inner route are shown. Wherever the path passes through identical shapes in each grid, the route of the path must be exactly the same, although it may be rotated and/or reflected relative to the other grid.

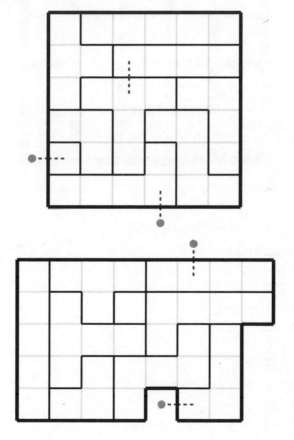

(24) APT PROPERTY 2

In what way do the letters in the word EQUATION form an equation?

(25) DIGITALLY ENHANCED JIGSAW

Solve the clues, which are arranged alphabetically in order
of their full solution. Enter them where they fit, so as to fill
the crossword grid. Bars indicate the ends of entries.

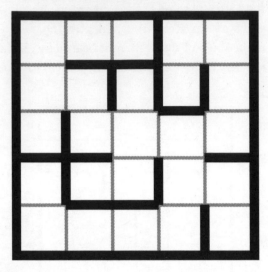

Whichever (2)
Earlier (2)
Not harmful (2)
Dog (2)
Stray (3)
What's seized in Latin (2)
Waste away (4)
Arise (3)
Pictogram (3)
Scientific crime department (3)
Horse (2)
Shortest lines between points (4)
S-shaped moulding (2)
An essential amino acid (3)
French river and department (2)

(26) ODD PAIR OUT 2

The following twelve words can be divided into six pairs.
Which is the odd pair out?

▶ Absent

▶ Boar

▶ Bucks

▶ Darkness

▶ Demand

▶ Distant

▶ Heavy

▶ Open

▶ Reap

▶ Receive

▶ Rigidly

▶ Undoes

(27) POP SUMS 2

If Elvis Presley + Coldplay + Radiohead + Prince = Right Said
Fred, then complete the following equations:

▶ Spice Girls + Olivia Newton-John + Adele + Kenny Ball &
His Jazzmen = _____

▶ _____ + Spandau Ballet + Commodores +
Sweet = _____

(28) GRIDFILL 3

Fill the grid below with letters, one to each square, in such a way that each one of the seven sages of Greece – BIAS, CHILON, CLEOBULUS, PERIANDER, PITTACUS, SOLON and THALES – can be traced by starting at a letter and moving through adjacent squares horizontally and vertically, but not diagonally. Double letters must occupy two adjacent squares, and squares can be revisited within a word. To help you, two identical configurations of four letters have been marked with shaded squares.

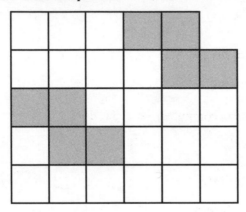

(29) ALPHABETIC EXTRACTION

There are three different keys on a key ring: a car key, a house key and a factory key. Unfortunately, the owner has forgotten which key unlocks each item, but luckily there is some writing on each key, as shown below. Can you work out which key, when correctly inserted, unlocks each item?

▶ Key 1: V K N G P B K L

▶ Key 2: C U T N L N A H K D

▶ Key 3: P E Q D S E K U E

(30) FIND THE ACTRESS

Solve the clues and find the actress:

▶ Angled

▶ Baby's shoe

▶ Body louse

▶ Curbed

▶ Mountainside basin (Scot)

▶ Punched

▶ Scrounged (Aust)

▶ Soccer

▶ Started up (a computer)

▶ To potter

▶ To snuggle (Scot)

▶ Town near Liverpool

▶ Was of the correct size

Hints

Every puzzle has at least one hint, but most puzzles have several. They are intended to be read one-by-one in order, so when you are stuck on a puzzle, read just the first hint and see if it helps. If you remain stuck, then return and read the second hint, and then so on and so on for the remainder of the hints until you — hopefully — make progress on the puzzle.

HINTS FOR CHAPTER I: DECIPHERABLE

(I) FLOWER POWER

▶ Flower Power/flowery language means there is something to do with flowers in each sentence
▶ Each sentence contains the name of a flower hidden within the text

(2) MOVIE EDITS

▶ These are strange phrases –what could be going on?
▶ They are anagrams of movie titles

(3) WORD CONNECTIONS

▶ The first column is FIRE ARM BAND, creating the terms FIREARM and ARMBAND
▶ The missing word on the right is MAN

(4) END OF SERIES

▶ Everything you need to know is on the page
▶ Take a look at the words asking the question
▶ Consider the final letters

(5) WHAT THE...?

▶ The title is a clue – what comes next in that phrase?
▶ What is missing from the characters listed?
▶ There are no vowels – you must restore them
▶ They are Dickens characters

(6) CLOCK SCHEDULING

▶ This requires historical knowledge, which you could look up online or in a reference book
▶ Each line refers to a battle
▶ Each time refers to a year

(7) COMPLETE THE PICTURE

▶ The same letters are missing from each line
▶ The title is a clue

(8) PUNAGRAMS I

▶ The first letter to remove is S
▶ The first country is famous for chocolate and Hercule Poirot
▶ The second letter to remove is P
▶ The third letter to remove is R
▶ The fourth letter to remove is A

(9) TETRA-DROP GRID FILL

▶ Piece 1 could fit in one of four positions, but it can't go on the far left or else piece 2 couldn't fit
▶ Once you place piece 1, piece 2 must fit onto piece 1, either off the left or on top of it, otherwise there'd be a gap below
▶ You need to spell words too, so experiment with how piece 3 can fit
▶ Once you have the first few pieces placed, the rest is straightforward
▶ Piece 1 goes at the bottom right
▶ Piece 2 goes in columns 3 and 4
▶ Piece 3 goes in columns 1 and 2

(10) ANAGRAM CONNECTIONS I

▶ The first anagram solution starts with CO____
▶ The fifth anagram starts with PL_____
▶ The final anagram starts with MA____
▶ What word can go before or after each solved anagram?

(11) TABLE OF RIVERS

▶ Why is it a 'table' of rivers?
▶ What tables can you think of that use numbers, like here?
▶ Look at the first one or two letters of each entry. What do these remind you of?
▶ Consult the Periodic Table

(12) QUOTE HANJIE

▶ This puzzle can be solved with pure logic – no guessing needed. The key thing to do is to mark squares that are definitely part of the quote, as well as squares that are definitely shaded

▶ You can cross-reference deductions back and forth between rows and columns until the puzzle is solved

▶ Row 1, when shaded, leaves THOSE

▶ Row 2, when shaded, leaves WHOCAN

▶ The final row, when shaded, leaves IBLE

(13) PUNAGRAMS 2

▶ The first anagram starts with C

▶ The first anagram starts CO____

▶ The second anagram starts A

▶ The second anagram starts AR___

(14) COMMON FEATURES I

▶ They are strange phrases – why?

▶ They are anagrams

▶ They are anagrams of the same kind of thing

▶ The last one ends with 'ton'

(15) ANAGRAM CONNECTIONS 2

▶ The first anagram is DANCE

▶ The seventh anagram starts TR____

▶ You're looking for a word that can go before or after each anagram

▶ It's a five-letter word starting with F

(16) ODD NAME OUT I

▶ Why does it mention Oscar?

▶ Are these just names, or is there another connection too?

▶ It refers to the Oscars – the movie awards

▶ They are all names of movies

(17) COMMON FEATURES 2

▸ The 'reference' referred to is a dictionary
▸ What do you spot in common between the definitions?
▸ What can you 'derive' – what derivations are in a dictionary?
▸ Where do the words come from?

(18) THE VAULT

▸ There is an 'X' on the left. There aren't many words of the form 'EX__'.
▸ There also aren't many that read 'EW__'
▸ Can you find a rotation of the dials that makes words for both of these?

(19) WHERE AM I?

▸ How many times is 'SE' repeated in the first one?
▸ Try saying the count and 'SE' out loud
▸ They are rebuses – words represented by combinations of sounds from letters and pictures
▸ The first one is ten SE
▸ The first one is Tennessee
▸ The second has 'ILL' inside 'OIS'
▸ The third is a picture of a road followed by what?
▸ The fourth is an 'M' on some letters
▸ The fifth is an anagram
▸ For the fifth, a way of cluing an anagram is to say 'new'
▸ The penultimate one is written right-to-left

(20) WATCH THIS

▸ Why is it called 'Watch This'?
▸ It refers to movie titles
▸ What is missing from the titles?

(21) COMMON FEATURES 3

▸ Can you think of some synonyms of the words?
▸ Can you find two synonyms of each word?
▸ Can you find two contrasting synonyms of each word?

(22) CAN YOU CONNECT I

▶ There is something you can do to all these things

(23) ALTERNATIVE EXPRESSIONS I

▶ What does the first entry remind you of?
▶ Think of the title
▶ Think of common expressions

(24) ANAGRAM CONNECTIONS 3

▶ You're looking for a word that can go either before or after all of the solved anagrams

(25) SIX MIX I

▶ The first line is an anagram of KINDLE
▶ And the second is an anagram of STREAM
▶ The other anagrams are IMPURE, CURATE, PORTAL and CAMPED

(26) COMMON FEATURES 4

▶ Strange phrases – why?
▶ These are anagrams of something
▶ The first word of the first one is King
▶ And the second word of the first one is Lear

(27) KEY NUMBERS

▶ What is a 'key number'?
▶ Or, more particularly, what is a 'number key'?
▶ It's on a keyboard
▶ What else is on the number?

(28) CONNECTION I

▶ What country does 'cafetière' hail from?
▶ What is an alternative name for a cafetière?
▶ Can you think of a type of salad accompaniment?
▶ And what is eggy bread called?
▶ Another word for chips is... what?
▶ What is the common term?

(29) LITERARY SET

- ▸ How is it a 'literary set'?
- ▸ The connection is books
- ▸ Each book has been modified in some way
- ▸ Can you guess at any of the original titles? What has changed?
- ▸ The first title should be The Crow Road
- ▸ How does Murder connect to Crow?
- ▸ The second title should be H is for Hawk

(30) MOVIE CLUB I

- ▸ Do these look a bit like real movie titles?
- ▸ What has changed in each case?
- ▸ The first one should be Charlie Wilson's War
- ▸ What connects Wilson to Harding?
- ▸ The second should be King Arthur

(31) OBSCENE TITLES

- ▸ What can you spot in common between all the titles?
- ▸ Why is the puzzle called 'obscene titles'?
- ▸ Do the titles remind you of real movie or book titles?
- ▸ The first should be Ocean's Eleven
- ▸ What is another term for an obscene movie?

(32) MOVIE CLUB 2

- ▸ Do these remind you of real movie titles?
- ▸ What has changed?
- ▸ The first should be Jackie Brown
- ▸ What connects Blair to Brown?
- ▸ The second should be East of Eden

(33) PUNAGRAMS 3

- ▸ The first letter to remove is T
- ▸ The second to remove is W
- ▸ The third and fourth are O and L respectively
- ▸ The fifth and sixth are I and P respectively

(34) RADICAL TITLES

- ▶ What can you spot in common between the titles?
- ▶ They are movies, plays, books and songs
- ▶ The first should be Ruby Tuesday
- ▶ The second should be Crimson Tide
- ▶ What do Ruby and Rose have in common?

(35) NAVIGRID I

- ▶ The '1 left and 2 down' tile can only be used in a single place, forcing the position of the 8
- ▶ The two '2 down' tiles must then be used to move from 6 to 7, and from 1 to 2
- ▶ The '1 up and 1 right' tile now only has one place it can be used, to move from the leftmost square to the first square on the top row
- ▶ Now you can use the '1 up' tile, since there's only one place it can be used

(36) AGENT ACTIVITY

- ▶ The key word is 'created' – you are not looking for a connection, but a way to link the words together
- ▶ Dracula is a Count
- ▶ What is Ireland often called in poetry?
- ▶ Ireland is often called Erin
- ▶ What happens if you link those two words together?
- ▶ Place them in order – you are spelling something out

(37) LATELY LONGING

- ▶ Look at the title. Does it contain a clue?
- ▶ In what way are numbers sometimes associated with countries?
- ▶ Think about positions
- ▶ What are the first three letters of each word in the title?

(38) CONNECTION 2

- ▶ Slander is defamation
- ▶ A Muslim woman's headdress is a hijab
- ▶ The third answer starts with 'n'

▶ The last two answers start with 's' and 't' respectively
▶ Look at the words you now have
▶ What can you spot in common between their letters?

(39) TRAVEL TEST

▶ Anagrams are involved
▶ What could 'open change' be an anagram of?
▶ It starts with C
▶ It starts with COP_____
▶ It is an anagram of Copenhagen
▶ How does that connect to the question?

(40) FEATURE I

▶ Try saying them out loud
▶ Is there a common aural feature?

(4I) SWAP AND SWITCH

▶ The first letter to add is O
▶ The first letter to remove is E
▶ The first word starts with C
▶ The first word is CORSET

(42) GLOBETROTTING I

▶ Where have I been? How are US cities often written?
▶ Why is that song called 'New York, New York'?
▶ What states are the cities in?
▶ Each state has a two-character abbreviation

(43) FEATURE 2

▶ Try saying them out loud
▶ What is the common spoken feature?

(44) ALPHAHUNT I

▶ You can find jealousy and exercise in the puzzle
▶ And also burglar, wrinkle, uniform and quartz
▶ Plus also violence, charge and medium

(45) IN OTHER WORDS

- ▶ It is a paraphrased story
- ▶ A nursery rhyme, to be precise

(46) CAN YOU CONNECT 2

- ▶ There is something you can be said to do to all of them
- ▶ You can ___ a fire, ____ an exam, ____ a clock, etc

(47) SPOT THE LINK I

- ▶ You're looking for something in common with the words as given
- ▶ Look closely
- ▶ Look at the letters

(48) SIX MIX 2

- ▶ The first line is an anagram of ASTUTE
- ▶ And the second is an anagram of REMOTE
- ▶ The other anagrams are DECREE, CIRCLE, DAMPER and TRAVEL

(49) SPOT THE LINK 2

- ▶ Try saying them out loud
- ▶ Now try saying them out loud again...
- ▶ This time, do it differently
- ▶ What do they mean?
- ▶ Do they have multiple meanings?

(50) CAN YOU CONNECT 3

- ▶ What can you 'do' to all of them?
- ▶ You can ___ a cold

(5I) REBUSES

- ▶ The first line is a face
- ▶ And a book
- ▶ Face... book
- ▶ The second line is ROPE with a gap in the middle
- ▶ It's been cut into two
- ▶ The third line is lots of 3s

- ▶ The first three entries are Facebook, Cut the Rope and Threes
- ▶ What is in common between them all?
- ▶ The final entry has 'STAG' written around the outside

(52) STRIP SEARCH

- ▶ Why is it called 'strip search'?
- ▶ At each step the answer is 'stripped'
- ▶ The band of buccaneers are pirates
- ▶ You now know all you need to know! Read the above again!

(53) MUSIC MIX

- ▶ 'Re-mixed' indicates anagrams – they are anagrams of song titles and their artists
- ▶ The first one is by an artist with initials M T
- ▶ The first one is by Meghan Trainor
- ▶ The last one is by an artist with initials W H
- ▶ The last one is by Whitney Houston

(54) SPORTS FILL

- ▶ There are three entries in a row, in the 13th, 14th and 15th rows, that end in the same four letters
- ▶ They must end in 'BALL'
- ▶ The second letter of one of them overlaps with the first or fourth letter of three other words – this helps you make a couple of deductions
- ▶ The 13th entry is HANDBALL
- ▶ Carry on using similar logic

(55) GEM OF A PUZZLE

- ▶ What is a 'gem'?
- ▶ What type of thing is it?
- ▶ What is made up of pounds?

(56) CAPITAL LETTERS

- ▶ What do the _ - _ _ _ _ etc entries on the right mean?

▶ What is the hyphen for?

▶ You are looking for hyphenated words

▶ The number of letters is shown

▶ Look for solutions to the clues. The first is B-movie

▶ What is the title again?

▶ Look at all the initial letters

57 ONE MORE LETTER

▶ The first letter to add is S

▶ The second to add is T

▶ The first word begins with L

▶ The second word begins with S

58 LINK WORDS

▶ The first link word begins with B

▶ The second begins with D

▶ The third begins with S

▶ The fourth begins with D

▶ The first link word is BASKET

59 LATIN PAIRS

▶ Solve these Latin grids using sudoku skills – for each row and column, see if there is only one place a particular letter or number will fit

▶ The first letter row is VKTLMW

▶ The first number row is 126534

60 DROP ZONE

▶ Delete L from the first row up to make CUISINE

▶ This now gives you 'ICEBRRG' in the second row up

▶ So delete the first R to make ICEBERG

▶ This gives you STYLIET in the third row up

▶ Which should be STYLIST

HINTS FOR CHAPTER 2:
COMPUTABLE

(1) GOING IN BLIND

- ▶ Why is it called 'Going in blind'?
- ▶ The grid entries are mostly fairly short... shorter than the clue lengths given, in fact
- ▶ The solution to the first clue is DIGIT
- ▶ The solution to the third clue is FINISH
- ▶ The solution to the fifth clue is HITCH-HIKING
- ▶ What do you spot in common between the solutions?
- ▶ If you are blind, what do you lack?
- ▶ What do these words have in abundance?
- ▶ What if they lacked that thing? How would they appear then? Would they be short enough to fit in the grid?

(2) PIVOT POINTS

- ▶ Most of the words, but not all, can also be read backwards
- ▶ This isn't the answer, but it's quite close – what does 'Pivot points' refer to?
- ▶ What if you 'pivot' the word on its final letter?

(3) HOLY ORDERS

- ▶ 'Confused' indicates anagrams
- ▶ What is the 'holy' order?

(4) MAN TO MAN

- ▶ ROB changes first of all to MUG
- ▶ And if you are mugging, you are...
- ▶ ...fooling around – so MUG changes to FOOL
- ▶ To fool around is to josh about, so the first one is finished
- ▶ The second puzzle changes first of all to an anagram of the given word
- ▶ The third puzzle goes first to a four-letter word that starts with a J

▶ The fourth puzzle goes first to a four-letter word starting with S

⑤ A NEW TERM

▶ Try writing the numbers out in words
▶ What do you spot, initially?

⑥ CAN YOU CONNECT 4

▶ You can do something to all of them
▶ You can ___ a curtain, for example

⑦ ROUTE SUM

▶ The Battle of Hastings took place in which year?
▶ Look up the other events. What years did they take place?
▶ So what is in common, and what is the sequence?

⑧ NAVIGRID 2

▶ The '1 left and 1 down' must be used to escape from the top square in the rightmost column, if it's not the 9
▶ There are only two possible moves from the 7 – right 1 and down 1, and right 1 and down 2
▶ For each of those possible moves, what would come next?
▶ Experiment with possible routes, making pencil-mark notes of your deductions

⑨ MISFORTUNE

▶ Who was Millard Fillmore?
▶ What does lace celebrate?
▶ What number book is 'I Chronicles' in the King James Bible?

⑩ ENDEAVOUR TO SOLVE

▶ What common sequences can you spot?
▶ Who is called 'Endeavour'?
▶ What words appear frequently?
▶ And do they appear hidden within or across other words too?
▶ Break them down by sentence

- ▶ And then decode them
- ▶ You're looking for 'dash' and 'dot'

(11) ODD NAME OUT 2: VENGEANCE

- ▶ 'Vengeance' – what movie title ends with this?
- ▶ Marvel at this question

(12) ELEPHANT DEVICES

- ▶ EGBDF – something musical
- ▶ MVEMJSUNP – one-time space set
- ▶ BYRBG – sporty
- ▶ GELND – God is a clue!
- ▶ SHMEO – they're Great
- ▶ TGCFAOQTCD – this is hard; or about hardness, more properly
- ▶ CNLMDBC – who is the 'British Commander' they speak of?

(13) HIDDEN FLOWERS

- ▶ A flower can be pronounced differently...
- ▶ ...as a 'flow-er', i.e. a river
- ▶ You're looking for hidden rivers in the sentences
- ▶ One of the rivers is the Po – congratulations if you managed to spot that without a hint!
- ▶ The others begin with C, N, O and T

(14) PISCINE PHRASES

- ▶ You're looking for hidden water creatures
- ▶ The first one is 'bleak'
- ▶ The third entry has four hidden in it
- ▶ The last two have two each

(15) FEATURE 3

- ▶ Say them out loud
- ▶ Which bit of each don't you say?

(16) FOUR BY FOUR I

- ▶ The first solution is ASAP

▶ The second is TOPS
▶ The next three are REPS, EASE, TRAP
▶ And finally SETT, STAR, TARO
▶ The top-left letter is S

(17) TABLE OF COUNTRIES

▶ What are the numbers for?
▶ What sort of table does it refer to?
▶ Consult the Periodic Table

(18) KLUMP I

▶ The 5 goes at the bottom-left
▶ The 7 goes at the bottom-right
▶ The 12 goes at the top-left

(19) GLOBETROTTING 2

▶ Look for a way to convert each country to a letter sequence
▶ How might you journey around?
▶ Not by plane, but by car
▶ Look up international vehicle registrations for each country

(20) VENN I

▶ This is a very shapely question
▶ The letters on the left have no curves

(21) PUNAGRAMS 4

▶ The first two extra letters are J and U
▶ The second two are R and A
▶ The first anagram solution starts with S
▶ As does the second
▶ The first is SETTER
▶ The second is SAMOYED
▶ The third loses S and S

(22) ALPHAHUNT 2

▶ One word to find is fraction

▶ Two more are viper and squish
▶ Also aerobic, jerk, pillow
▶ And gnash, text, pretty
▶ And something with 'z' at the start

(23) ALWAYS ASK WHY

▶ Always ask what?
▶ Say it out loud
▶ Why?
▶ The count of what matches up with the numbers?

(24) WHO'S NEXT?

▶ The first entry is George
▶ The second is William
▶ The third is Victoria
▶ What sequence might this be?

(25) FEATURE 4

▶ Say them out loud
▶ Which bit don't you say?

(26) WALL TO WALL

▶ The first solution is DUVET
▶ The letters in the squares numbered 2 and 3 are T and H
▶ The letters in the squares numbered 4 and 5 are A and E
▶ The letters in the squares numbered 6 and 7 are R and E
▶ The letter in the square numbered 8 is S
▶ The final solution is STAG

(27) OBSCURE

▶ Think of the weather
▶ Look up, most days

(28) NEXT LINE

▶ It's a lyrical sequence i.e. lyrics from something..
▶ Something seasonal..
▶ ...that is played at Christmas

(29) WORD FUNKTION

- ▶ Why is 'funktion' spelled like that?
- ▶ It's a German spelling of 'function'
- ▶ Does the last phrase remind you of anything?
- ▶ It's described by a German word...
- ▶ ....that otherwise has no direct equivalent in English

(30) MUDDIED TITLES

- ▶ Each has had a hu(g)e shift
- ▶ The first should be Under Milk Wood
- ▶ The second should be Coffee Cantata

(31) DOUBLE DUTY NAMES

- ▶ They are capital cities of which countries?
- ▶ Why does it say 'names' in the title too?
- ▶ Some of them are Hungary, Denmark and Pakistan – what do these have in common?
- ▶ And what about Argentina, Rwanda and Bolivia?
- ▶ Look at the ends of the words

(32) IT'S ALL AN ACT

- ▶ You're looking for link words
- ▶ The first is toy
- ▶ The second is story
- ▶ The last one is atlas
- ▶ Once you have the link words, look down the list and what do you see?
- ▶ Does it remind you of anyone's career?
- ▶ What was the title again?

(33) QUESTION

- ▶ What is the title?
- ▶ The title is a massive hint
- ▶ Bits of each word are missing
- ▶ The start and end in fact

(34) DEPARTURES

- ▶ Take your time.... what does that mean?

▸ You can count on the destination.... in what way?

▸ You need to count the letters in the destination...

▸ ...using values derived from the time

▸ Take the difference between the hours and minutes

▸ And index into the city with it

▸ Then see what you've spelled out

(35) CAESAR'S FINAL MOVE

▸ They all looked 'shifty'

▸ Caesar... shifty

▸ Do you know what a Caesar shift is?

▸ Can you create a number from the text to give you a clue to the Caesar shift?

(36) ECOLOGICAL TITLES

▸ Ecological... or another word for that is... what?

▸ One hue is exchanged for another

▸ The first title should be Parsley Sage Rosemary and Thyme

▸ The second should be Midnight Express

(37) NUMERACY

▸ What is 'old numeracy'?

▸ Really old numbers are... what kind of numbers?

▸ Look at the letters in the words

▸ Do they conceal numbers of some kind?

▸ Numbers made from letters?

▸ Roman numbers?

(38) EVER-DECREASING CIRCLES

▸ There are 100 years in a century

▸ And the distance to a target in Olympic archery is 70m

▸ L is 50, in Roman numerals

▸ Why is 'Cats' Lives' upside down? Maybe the answer is too

▸ Each circle corresponds to a different number

▸ Trace a path...

▸ ...of ever-decreasing value

▸ You finish on the bottom-right circle

(39) STEPPING WITH STYLE

▶ The instructions are given in the question...
▶ ....but the dance is with the letters, not your feet
▶ So take steps with the first letter
▶ And then the second
▶ And then repeat the dance

(40) TANGLED DUOS

▶ The first is SALT and PEPPER
▶ The second is SONNY and?
▶ The third is a pair of star-crossed lovers

(41) HEADS OF STATE

▶ Heads... of state
▶ Where are there literal heads of state?
▶ Somewhere in the US, specifically
▶ Four in a row, in fact
▶ They're really large
▶ Carved into a mountainside, to be precise

(42) SAVAGE BRACKETS

▶ What are the brackets referred to in the title?
▶ The brackets are the groups of three items
▶ You're looking for a single entry that can go in front of each item in a group, in each place marked by an empty line
▶ So for example the topmost entry is GAME, to make GAMEBOY, GAMESHOW and GAME THEORY
▶ Now find similar solutions for the other groups
▶ And do the same with the results of groups to make new groups, until every empty line has a word on it

(43) SUPERMARKET SHENANIGANS

▶ How can you give words value?
▶ Or more specifically letters?
▶ Perhaps A=1, B=2, etc?

(44) VENN 2

▶ A lot of those numbers are even
▶ And some aren't

▶ But others have a certain property

▶ Think of squares

㊺ A STARTING CODE IS INVOLVED

▶ Hex refers to hexadecimal

▶ Look at the title

▶ What are its initials?

▶ What does that mean?

㊻ DEPECHE CODE

▶ Why are the tracks listed in that order?

▶ It isn't alphabetical

▶ What do the first letters of the tracks spell out?

▶ Do what it says!

▶ For 'Isn't She lovely' by Stevie Wonder, the track length is
1 minute (and 38 seconds) so take letter 1 of the artist's
name, as indicated by '1 minute', to get 'S'

▶ What does this spell out?

▶ You have a three word instruction

▶ Then convert the resulting set of numbers into letters

▶ The final result is a pun

㊼ FOUR BY FOUR 2

▶ The first solution is FIVE

▶ The second is IDEA

▶ The next three are ESSE, VEST, LESS

▶ And finally FOLD, ODES, DATE

▶ The top-left letter is F

㊽ BEEPING MAD

▶ What communication method might beep?

▶ What is literally 'in' the text?

㊾ SECONDS AND THIRDS

▶ The title is key

▶ You have the seconds and thirds...

▶ ...of each word

▶ The first sequence is numbers

▶ It is oNE, tWO, tHRee, and so on
▶ The next is a calendar sequence
▶ Then we have something chemical
▶ Next up, we view the world as if through a prism...
▶ Then we take a trip through historical leaders
▶ Finally, we turn our gaze to the heavens

(50) BACKWORDS

▶ The title is important
▶ Some words are reversed
▶ Note that each 'becomes' something
▶ They are synonyms of words
▶ But the second one is reversed
▶ So STRAP (FASTEN)...
▶ ....becomes PARTS (ROLES)

(51) SCRATCH THAT

▶ I'm on the corner of a map
▶ And in slang it means to scratch a car or other item of value, as hinted at by the title
▶ It's a common ending to a place name in the Caribbean
▶ Of islands, to be specific

(52) ON DEAF EARS

▶ What part of each word is 'deaf'?
▶ What isn't pronounced in each word?
▶ Make a note of these parts
▶ What do they spell?
▶ How does this connect to the title?

(53) MIDDLESIX I

▶ The top-left letter is U
▶ The bottom-right letter is C
▶ The top-right letter is E
▶ The bottom-left letter is O

(54) COME AGAIN?

▶ What is the French dance?

- ▶ It's the can-can
- ▶ Why is the answer only three letters?
- ▶ Good vision is twenty-twenty vision
- ▶ Notice anything in common with the answers, and the space given for them in the puzzle?
- ▶ They're repeated
- ▶ What do the question marks mean?
- ▶ What might these letters spell out?

(55) SO IT BEGINS (AND ENDS)

- ▶ The title tells you pretty much what to do
- ▶ The first solution is CHURCH
- ▶ The second is INSULIN
- ▶ Can you spot the connection?

(56) ALTERNATIVE EXPRESSIONS 2

- ▶ The title is a big hint
- ▶ Amused can mean 'laughing'
- ▶ Part of a gun is a 'stock'
- ▶ Put them together
- ▶ Just can mean 'fair'
- ▶ Limping can mean 'lame'

(57) SPY LOGIC

- ▶ Use the grid to keep track of deductions, placing 'X's for combinations that are definitely wrong, and ticks for combinations that are correct
- ▶ Based on the first clue, tick the intersection of 'Kristina' and 'Karpova', and put 'X's for all other 'Kristina'+surname and 'Karpova'+first name options
- ▶ Kristina Karpova didn't have an electric toothbrush, so place an 'X' on the intersection of Kristina and 'toothbrush' in the grid, and of 'Karpova' and toothbrush

HINTS FOR CHAPTER 3: TESTING

(1) UK TRANSPORT PREDICTIONS

▶ The title is important, but it is up to you to decide what kind of UK transport it refers to

▶ It is to do with navigation, as hinted at by 'navigate a way'

▶ The table is called a 'chart' – why is that?

▶ One of the sets of three involves homophones

▶ The homophone set includes SOUL

▶ It also includes PHARAOHS

▶ Another one of the sets is anagrams

▶ One of the anagrams is GORGED

▶ And another anagram is FATTENS

▶ A third set is surnames of well-known figures – the first names form the required set

▶ A fourth set is UK geographical locations with the first word omitted – the omitted words form the required set

▶ The 12 items in this puzzle are in fact part of a set of 31

▶ They are sea areas, as used in UK shipping forecasts

(2) FIVE BY FOUR

▶ Each set is joined in a theme – there is no word play

▶ One set is to do with shades of a colour

▶ Another is to do with a classic arcade game

▶ One is slang terms

▶ Another involves edible things

▶ One of the sets includes INKY and CLYDE

▶ Another involves CHESTNUT and CHOCOLATE

▶ A third has PINS and NOODLE

(3) THE MAN WITH THE GOLDEN PUN

▶ Can you explain the title?

▶ How does it contrast with a more familiar title?

▶ What, precisely, has changed?

▶ One letter has been altered

▶ What movie series does the title (almost) come from?

▶ In the first title, what is the word for a female sheep?

▶ It is a ewe

▶ What is another word for 'solely'

▶ How about 'only'?

▶ Can you think of a title that ends with something similar to 'ewes only'?

▶ The title described here is 'For Your Ewes Only'...

▶ ....which is one letter away from 'For Your Eyes Only'

▶ All of the entries clue James Bond movie titles, with a single letter changed

④ NEXT IN LINE I

▶ The first sequence is out of this world

▶ The second is worth counting out

▶ The third is ancient

▶ The fourth and fifth are both timely

⑤ ESCAPED ANIMALS

▶ Unusual word choice in the clues often indicates the place an animal should go

▶ The first missing animal fits in the middle of 'dolly'

▶ The second fits in 'sis'

▶ The first missing animal is a lion

▶ The second is a zebra

▶ The third is a snake

▶ The fourth is a camel

▶ The fifth is a bear

⑥ DIVERSITY TEST

▶ The first is a book by Tom Clancy

▶ The second was made into a Kubrick movie

▶ What types of word occur in common between the two?

▶ So what do you think the sequence is?

(7) LIFE FORMS

▶ Can you find a property that all the first column share?
▶ They are all anagrams
▶ Then, can you find a property that all the unscrambled words share?

(8) KEY WORDS

▶ The key here is 'key'
▶ What types of key can you think of
▶ What about ones you hit with your fingers?

(9) SEQUENCE I

▶ Where is the Grand Canyon?
▶ Where are the rest?

(10) HOUSE–HUNTING

▶ This puzzle is based on a particular type of advanced cryptic crossword clue called DLM – definition and letter mixture – which you can look up online
▶ 'Wisdom, perhaps' is a clue for the answer in the first sentence, and it refers to a former English actor who was knighted in 2000
▶ 'Roman n' is its letter-mixture anagram
▶ The answer to this is 'Norman'
▶ This sentence then goes on to provide a clue to the next item – the question notes that some sentences contain more than one item
▶ 'given an' is the next letter-mixture anagram
▶ The next straight clue is 'an area of western France'

(11) FINAL AGENT

▶ What can you add ('final agent') to all the terms in each line?
▶ On the first line, you can add 'live' to each word
▶ The title is useful again, in checking you have the correct answer once you're done!

(12) WORD ASSOCIATION

▸ What could these numbers refer to?
▸ '41 and 43' is a pretty big clue
▸ What do the letters mean?
▸ The letters indicate changes from the immediate solution to each clue
▸ 'People' refers to 'folk'
▸ The solution to 'savage' is 'fierce'
▸ The solution to 'stream' is 'gush'
▸ You're looking for names of leaders

(13) THEMED PAIRS

▸ Try to make headway by seeking to find the word required by the more precise clues
▸ What could link a plant with orange or yellow heads and a 18th-century Irish dramatist?
▸ Once this pairing has been established, can you find others of a similar type?
▸ The plant is a marigold
▸ The glittering paper is tinsel

(14) MUSICAL WORDS

▸ What is a word for 'came to the throne'?
▸ And 'emotional problems'?
▸ What property do these share?
▸ In what way are they 'musical words'?
▸ What words could you write 'in music'?
▸ Each word has a peculiar property suggested by the title in terms of the range of letters that they use

(15) A BIT TO EAT

▸ The title is key
▸ Read the instructions out loud – do you hear any numbers?
▸ Each row corresponds to a letter
▸ Each letter is made up from 'bits'
▸ A bit is a binary digit
▸ A1.... A=1?

(16) VENN 3

▶ What is special about the set on the right?
▶ They happen to all be cities, but maybe that's not the key thing about this set
▶ What features are combined in the middle?

(17) EXTRA

▶ Where can you get cash from?
▶ What is the acronym for that machine?
▶ Reread the previous hint, with the acronym inserted
▶ Expand that acronym and write the sentence out – what do you spot?

(18) IT'S ALL GREEK TO ME

▶ Greek? In what way? Solve the clues to find English words
▶ How is the table of words used?
▶ Consider carefully the placement of components in a word
▶ Each word contains a Greek component
▶ What is an underground burial site called?
▶ And what is another word for a disaster? It's in the same set as the underground burial site solution
▶ The answer to 'suffering from an abnormality of movement and behaviour' is 'catatonic'

(19) AUTHORITATIVE COMMENTS

▶ What is missing from each line?
▶ A common type of letter is missing from each line
▶ Who makes 'authoritative comments'? Someone in authority?
▶ They are all quotations, with certain letters removed

(20) CLIMBER'S DIVISION

▶ 'Broadcast' is a cryptic way of saying 'sounds like'
▶ The singer is Prince
▶ The British naval college is Dartmouth

(21) PERIODIC PAIRS

▶ Periodic refers to time periods
▶ What can these act as prefixes to?

(22) BACK TO THE BEGINNING?

▶ This is a very well-known set, since its members generally hold wide influence
▶ The letters signify the names of people who have occupied a particular position based on a certain aspect of their name
▶ You have to determine which person is missing

(23) LEADERS OF THE GODS

▶ 'Leaders' is a hint to what you're looking for
▶ What is the 'leader' of 'Zeus'?
▶ Who does Zeus correspond to?
▶ Where does -16 come in?

(24) BILINGUAL GIBBERISH

▶ The expressions all share two properties
▶ Try using an online translation or search
▶ Each expression represents a different national way of expressing the same sentiment, using the same method

(25) PUNAGRAMS 5

▶ The pun question is very helpful!
▶ The first missing letter is L
▶ The second is A

(26) KLUMP 2

▶ The 7 is leftmost
▶ The 22 and the 14 are on the right-hand side
▶ The 8 is in the third column
▶ The 13 is in the 7th and 8th columns

(27) MISSION ACTIVITY

▶ How might you end up with 'leftovers'?
▶ You need to remove a letter from each

▶ Each word is then anagrammed so that all the resulting words share a common property

(28) STAGE

▶ The names are actors
▶ What are their first names?
▶ Is there a connection between these names and the plays?

(29) NUMBER SEQUENCE

▶ What happened in all those countries?
▶ When?
▶ Can you find a connection between the when and the number?

(30) TABLE OF CITIES

▶ What sort of table is this?
▶ How do the numbers connect?
▶ You might need a reference to find the answer, before you think of a suitable next item in the list

(31) PERSONAL CONNECTION

▶ What kind of 'personal connections' did they have?
▶ Who was their immediate family?
▶ Who did they succeed?

(32) LANGUAGE TOUR

▶ You may need to look up all or most of these online
▶ 'Monaco' in Italy does not translate to Monaco in the south of France, but rather to Munich in Germany
▶ There is no connection to find here – just a series of trivia

(33) BOARD

▶ What comes on a board?
▶ What is an 'outstanding' feature?
▶ What could 'outstand' from each line?
▶ It's a cryptic clue to remove a letter from each...
▶ ....and these removed letters can be rearranged to spell another item that fits with the rest

- ▶ The first letter to remove is 'e'
- ▶ Then rearrange the letters of 'crud' to make another word

(34) MIDDLESIX 2

- ▶ The top-left letter is A, and the bottom-right letter is I
- ▶ The other corners contain Es

(35) SEQUENCE 2

- ▶ These are nicknames
- ▶ Official, well-known nicknames for certain territories
- ▶ How do they connect, geographically?

(36) ALAN'S CURIOUS QUEST

- ▶ 'Alan's curious' is a clue – what could 'curious' mean?
- ▶ Try looking up the phrases
- ▶ They are chapter titles in a series of books...
- ▶ ....which has its own chronology
- ▶ Can you convert the books and chapters into coordinates?
- ▶ Plot them on the chart, relative to row 1 and column 1
- ▶ What do you see?

(37) FANDE

- ▶ What does the title mean? It's a big clue
- ▶ You're looking for a common prefix to one part of each line...
- ▶ ...that connects with the other part of the line

(38) SEQUENCE 3

- ▶ They are literary passages, as it says, and you will need to know the titles of the books they come from
- ▶ What sequence is demonstrated by the titles?

(39) EVEN MORE TANGLED DUOS

- ▶ The first is YIN and YANG
- ▶ The second is a pair of silent-movie comedians

(40) GO WITH THE FLOW

- ▶ What countries do these come from?
- ▶ What is the 'flow' the title speaks of?

(41) TRANSFORMATION

▶ Does 'liberty cabbage' remind you of 'liberty fries'? Perhaps there is a connection in their usage?

▶ Is there another term for 'Alsatian'?

(42) TYPES

▶ What do you know about the former pop singer, Prince?

▶ What about Oslo?

▶ And Gmail, in the UK?

(43) MINI BARRED CROSSWORD

▶ The crossword is too small to fit in the full answers

▶ You need to shorten your solutions to enter them

▶ The English county in 1-across is Essex

▶ And the composition in 1-down is an essay

▶ But 'E' is not the letter you enter in the square with the '1' in it

(44) EXCHANGE

▶ Why is the title 'exchange'? It's a big clue!

▶ How can you 'create' an extra word – by extracting letters perhaps?

▶ Remove one letter from each line...

▶ ....and unscramble the remaining letters on each line to make new words, then do the same with the extracted letters

(45) STATE YOUR NAME

▶ You might need to experiment a little here – try joining up names and seeing if you can find a connection

▶ One pair is Blaise Attlee

▶ Another is Klaus Tindall

(46) A LAKE IN A COUNTRY?

▶ The title is a cryptic crossword clue

▶ The country in the title is Austria, but the puzzle is not about Austria

▶ What could 'all directions bar East' be a clue to?

▶ It is a clue to NSW

㊼ ISOLATE I

▶ Draw a horizontal line in the middle of the second row of lines
▶ Then turn the area above it into one of your '5' regions
▶ There is then only one way to complete the region that connects to the top-right square...
▶ ...which must be the other '5' region
▶ The rightmost two squares on the bottom line are in the same region

㊽ TV PUZZLE

▶ Martin is in the art gallery
▶ The 7:15pm slot is 4 minutes long
▶ The 5 minute slot is about the large cat

㊾ TWO'S COMPANY I

▶ 'Two's company' is a hint...
▶ ....to pair the words
▶ You can form pairs which make compound words
▶ One word will be left over, since it can't form any pairs
▶ An example pair is HORSE + RADISH for HORSERADISH

㊿ FEATURE 5

▶ Try saying them out loud
▶ Is there a bit you don't say?

⑤ⓘ CONNECTION CLICHÉ

▶ 'Cliché' is a clue
▶ What is 'staircase wit'? Can you find a word for that?
▶ Try other languages

㊾ FEATURE 6

▶ Say them out loud
▶ Is there something you didn't say in each case?

HINTS FOR CHAPTER 4: ENCRYPTED

(I) BLETCHLEY PARK CROSSWORD

▶ The clues in this puzzle are solved as in a regular UK cryptic crossword. If you are unfamiliar with the rules and logic of cryptic crosswords then the main thing to bear in mind is that *every* clue includes a definition of the answer – it may be a somewhat misleading definition, but it is always there. The definition always makes up either the start or the end of the clue – never the middle – although it may occasionally also be the entire clue. The non-definition part of the clue is then made up of one or more cryptic indicators, for which you can find many books and online tutorials to explain the rules and logic – and all of the cryptic indicators in the clues in this puzzle are explained in the solutions

▶ The comment about perimeter squares means that the outermost letters on the borders of the grid will spell something (or, in fact, two things) when the puzzle is completed

(2) COMMON FEATURES 5

▶ Each item must be replaced with a synonym
▶ The four synonyms then share a property
▶ The synonym of 'untied' is 'loose'

(3) TIKTAKA I

▶ The same shape in each grid has the same path route through it, so start by copying from one grid to the other any shape entrances or exits that are already given – although for some of the shapes you may not be sure of the orientation of the shape in the other grid, you can still make a note that the path must pass through one of a certain set of points

▶ If a shape is against the edge of the grid in one grid, you know the path can't pass through that edge of it in the other grid so mark in bold borders to show where the path *can't* go

▶ Work back and forth between grids, copying potential path extensions to the other grid to see if it remains plausible, given the requirement to enter and exit each shape exactly once

▶ In the first grid, the path travels from the top-left square across to the fourth column before turning down

▶ In the second grid, the path travels straight up the first column to the top row, then across to the fifth column and then down

(4) WELCOME TO PUZZLANDIA

▶ Each of these puzzles results in a single word, so if after solving them you *don't* yet have a single word then you know you aren't finished! And you'll know if you're correct, without checking the solutions, because you'll get to use the answers from the previous puzzles to solve a final puzzle – so, if you want a tough challenge, you could try solving this entire series of puzzles without checking the solutions until the very end

▶ The final word will be relevant to the puzzle in some way, providing some inherent confirmation that you are correct

▶ In this puzzle, you will almost certainly need external help to make use of the numbers. An online search engine that specializes in numbers such as Wolfram Alpha is a good choice

▶ The title of this puzzle is Power Up – this is very important

▶ Powers of numbers are the key to this puzzle

▶ Each number is of the form x^y, so for example 16,777,216 = 2^{24} – that is, 2 to the power of 24

- ▶ The numbers given represent 1 to 8, each to various powers
- ▶ Deducing each power is the key to this puzzle
- ▶ Remember that the solution word is relevant to the puzzle
- ▶ The first power cannot be deduced, however, since $1^y = 1$ for all values of y
- ▶ Replace powers with letters, where 1=A, 2=B, 3=C, etc
- ▶ The first letter in the solution is E
- ▶ The second letter is X

⑤ *** OFF!

- ▶ The title is a critical part of the puzzle – and it is not intended to be offensive
- ▶ Each line has two clues – a punny clue on the left, as indicated by the question mark, and a straight clue on the right
- ▶ A number of letters is given in each case, one of which is highlighted with a question mark, so for example ? _ _ _ indicates a four-letter word
- ▶ The aim of this puzzle is to make two-word phrases...
- ▶ ...where each two-word phrase ends with the same word
- ▶ That word is not given in the number of letters breakdown, since it is to be repeated throughout
- ▶ Each phrase ends in 'OFF', as indicated by the title
- ▶ So 'Mozzarella-eating contest?' represents CHEESE OFF, which also means to annoy
- ▶ Extract the letter E from 'CHEESE OFF', as indicated by the question mark
- ▶ What do the letters spell out?
- ▶ Are you done? Remember the answer is a single word
- ▶ Imagine a question mark after the second word in the extracted text, as per the form of each line in the puzzle

⑥ FEEL LIKE A MEGA HERO

- ▶ What do you think the numbers around the puzzle mean?
- ▶ This is a logic problem, at least initially
- ▶ As always, the title is really important

▶ What might you 'feel'?

▶ Does the arrangement of the circles remind you of anything?

▶ You need to create something that could be felt by shading some of the dots

▶ Shade the dots in a way that corresponds to the number clues

▶ A circled number inside a box tells you how many dots to shade in that box

▶ Numbers at the ends of rows and columns reveal the total number of shaded dots in that row or column *in the corresponding position*

▶ So the '4' in the third box down on the right indicates that the bottom-left dot in all four boxes on that row must be shaded

▶ Cross out dots that must be empty based on the '0's

▶ Have you worked out what you're creating yet? It's a communication method that works by touch...

▶ ...and it's Braille

▶ You'll need to find a reference chart of Braille to letter conversions

▶ Braille is designed to be felt so what does this tell you about the patterns of dots, which you can also observe from a Braille-to-letter chart?

▶ There can never be an empty first row, or an empty first and second row, or an empty first column – this 'absence of anything' would not be possible to feel

▶ Once you have all the Braille letters, read off a message and answer the trivia question, which reveals an answer that connects back to the puzzle theme and its title

(7) ON THE WAY

▶ You need to work out what each picture represents

▶ What connection can you find between the words for each picture?

▶ Once you have found the connection, you can then be sure of the exact meaning of each picture

▶ The first picture is a COIN

- ▶ The second picture is a SOCK
- ▶ The third represents HONK
- ▶ Each picture translates to a four-letter word
- ▶ Each picture has some dots, dashes and slashes beneath – what are these?
- ▶ There is Morse code under each picture, but it doesn't yet make sense
- ▶ You need to rearrange the pictures in some way
- ▶ All the tiles are identical in shape, except a start and an end tile – they must be connected in a particular sequence
- ▶ There are a lot of similarities between words aren't there?
- ▶ Could DICE go next to RICE, and then RICE go next to RACE?
- ▶ You're forming a word ladder, where the next word in the ladder differs from the previous word by one letter
- ▶ Form the sequence of twenty words, starting with COIN and ending with FIRE
- ▶ Now it's time to use the Morse. The slashes represent gaps between letters
- ▶ One character has six dots or dashes. Have you looked up Morse punctuation?
- ▶ What does the Morse message say? Is it a single word? Are you finished?
- ▶ Remember the theme of the puzzle and apply it to the decoded Morse message

(8) PASSWORD

- ▶ A strange poem, that appears to contain instructions
- ▶ Have you read this poem out loud?
- ▶ According to the poem itself, how is the password encoded?
- ▶ It says it's encoded in a 'poetic scheme'
- ▶ Do you know anything about poetic schemes? If not, do some research
- ▶ Try searching for 'poetic scheme' or 'rhyme scheme'
- ▶ A poetic/rhyme scheme lists which lines rhyme with each other, using letters of the alphabet starting from A for

the first rhyme, B for the second rhyme, and onwards. For instance, a limerick has the rhyme scheme AABBA

▶ Try applying a rhyme scheme to this puzzle. The first line will have the rhyme scheme letter A. The second line will have the letter B, as it doesn't rhyme with the first line

▶ Now, the third line would normally have the rhyme scheme letter C. But what does the poem say about that?

▶ Use the letter R for the third line instead

▶ The fourth line rhymes with the first line, so therefore it has the rhyme scheme letter A

▶ The fifth line doesn't rhyme with anything else so far, so use the first unused letter of the alphabet for this line. Give it rhyme scheme letter C

▶ The sixth line rhymes with the first and fourth lines, so this has the letter A

▶ The seventh line doesn't rhyme with anything so far, so give that line the letter D

▶ Continue with each line, giving it the same letter rhyme scheme as anything else it rhymes with

▶ You've reached the end of the poem. Now what? Could those rhyme schemes come in useful?

▶ Spell out the rhyme schemes you've written for this poem

▶ The rhyme scheme letters spell out the password – you'll know if you have it right, when you read it!

⑨ WHAT'S THE META?

▶ This is a meta-puzzle which uses the five single-word answers you've already found so far. You might therefore find out that you don't have the final answer to one or more of the previous puzzles at this stage!

▶ But assuming you have all or most of the answers correct, then those letters on the ground should look familiar – compare them against your answer words

▶ Try navigating from start to finish spelling out the words you've found so far

▶ What do the letters you've not used say, when read in normal reading order?

▶ The letters you've not used say 'Look at the path you have taken'

▶ It's quite a windy path. How about breaking it into different sections?

▶ Each section should be one answer word from one puzzle

▶ The paths should now look like letters. What do they spell out?

▶ In answer order, and also from start to finish, they spell out the solution word

(10) NEXT IN LINE 2

▶ Each line is a set of initials

▶ One set is pretty to look at; another you can count on; one is something elemental; another is key; and the other is best typed out yourself

(11) KEYWORDS

▶ They are substitutions a machine might make in a certain situation

▶ But not so much nowadays, as it says

▶ On a phone keyboard, are there multiple letters on each number key?

(12) MIXING PAINT

▶ The word 'rails' is in quotes for a reason, and what's this about a fence? You might try doing some research on these words and how they might relate to a hidden message

▶ Why are there 'three' rails, and 'three' paints?

▶ You'll know if you decode the message successfully because you'll end up with three paints – using three rails

▶ Look up 'rail fence cipher'

(13) STILL ON THE ROAD

▶ Strange, out of context words? You've seen this before in this book!

▶ They are anagrams

▶ They are anagrams of cities

(14) MINI 5×5 JIGSAW

▶ The text 'arranged alphabetically in order of their full solution' is important to note since it will help

▶ The answers are really short, aren't they?

▶ You need to compress each answer in some way to fit to the letter lengths given, as is hinted at by the reference to a 'full solution'

▶ The first clue suggests 'Are you okay?' – so how would you write that in four letters?

▶ Spell each answer phonetically using letter pronunciations, so 'Are you okay?' becomes RUOK, and so on

(15) TWO BOYS

▶ Think carefully about the title of each category and its possible significance

▶ The headings give hints as to how each column is grouped

▶ There are five members to find – one per row, so each has three clues of three consistent kinds

▶ 'Echo' group suggests the use of sound

▶ 'Breakdown' group suggests the use of components

▶ 'Type' group suggests the use of items as illustrations of the groups to which they might belong

▶ For 'tree pitch', think of how you might pronounce the name of a tree and another word meaning pitch

▶ For 'award a hectare', think how the phrase could be split into its component parts – an abbreviation for a historic British award, then 'a', and then the abbreviation for hectare

▶ For 'Diana', think of what category of things the name might fall into and then think of another name in the same category that tallies with the answer provided by clues in the same row

▶ You need to work along each row horizontally to see how each item in the group could be separately defined

▶ There is a noted event to which all the answers refer in the same way – the title provides a cryptic hint to its location, although one that will only really provide confirmation once solved

▶ 'Tree pitch' is solved as tree=yew and pitch=tar

▶ 'Award a hectare' solves to award=OM, a=a and hectare=ha

▶ 'Diana' refers to the Roman goddess – so the overall answer for this row is also a Roman goddess

(16) GC&CS KEYWORD CYPHER

▶ The title is important – you need to work out what GC&CS refers to, in the context of this book

▶ And it is worth noting that CYPHER is spelled as 'CIPHER' elsewhere in this book

▶ Look at each code and try to establish what might stand for letters such as vowels that tend to occur with high frequency – the code word used to determine the cipher should slowly become apparent

▶ You need to create a keyword cipher based on the expansion of GC&CS, then decode the text using it

(17) WAVE DOWN

▶ The strange language in the question is there for a reason

▶ A 'ripest mix-up'? What might that refer to?

▶ 'Flag up' what is happening...

▶ A 'cross' that 'may be a sign', with something to 'calculate'?

▶ Have a look at the flags for the given countries

▶ You're doing flag mathematics

▶ A 'ripest' mix-up is a 'stripe' – so stripes are important

▶ You have three solved examples to demonstrate how the stripes and mathematical operators work

(18) OPERATIONS

▶ 'The clues also provide openings to an additional hint' is telling you that there's an extra clue written at the start of the clues...

▶ ...in the initial letters

▶ Each clue is a regular UK-style cryptic crossword clue –
see puzzle 1 of this chapter for some general advice on
solving cryptic crossword clues

▶ The shaded column will spell a thirteenth item of a set of
which you will by then already have twelve items, and this
thirteenth item is hinted at by the initial letters of the
clues

(19) STACKED TIPS

▶ Each answer increases in size by one letter, as does
the 'remainder of the word that *excludes* the common
property'

▶ Each answer shares a very particular property, which
should become apparent after you have solved one or two
answers

▶ The first clue, like all the rest, consists of a straight clue
for the entire answer, and a cryptic clue for the part that
excludes the common property – there are only two words
so there are only two ways to interpret it!

▶ 'Soprano' gives 'S', using a dictionary abbreviation

▶ 'Expert' gives 'hotshot'

(20) WORD SQUARE

▶ For the first property, consider each word carefully and
think what three letters could be inserted into each one
to form a new word

▶ For the second property, work out the way in which each
answer is presented and then apply the same treatment
to another word that could be defined by the others, once
the form of treatment has been deduced

▶ For the final property, think of a four-letter answer for
the first item and then add another letter each time for
subsequent answers – but note that only the first three
letters used in each answer are needed

▶ The name of the character can be read via a sequence
of horizontal and vertical moves in the word square –
including on one occasion moving in a reverse direction
to revisit a square

(21) FIESTA OF FUN

▶ What is the etymology of the word 'fiesta'?
▶ These phrases don't have single-word equivalences in English
▶ But they do in another language

(22) TRANSFORMATIONS

▶ A bucket is a pail
▶ Jump is leap, while a bell sound is a peal
▶ Look at the transformation in each case, and associate the transformation with the symbol
▶ A friend is a pal
▶ A force 8 wind is a gale, and a story is a tale
▶ Now apply the same transformations to the words given, one step at a time as shown
▶ There will be multiple ways to do this, but only one way that completes the chain of five commands *and* results in a word that matches one of the given clues

(23) NUMBER TRICK

▶ After multiplying, check the digits you have
▶ And specifically, how many different digits you have
▶ Check again after multiplying again
▶ Try writing out the digits that make up that second number in words

(24) SALVATION ARMY RANKS

▶ List A has some entries that are redolent of well-known places – particularly 'Good airs', 'Assumption' and 'The peace'
▶ For list A, find place names that can be formed by translating each item from English into a local language – in other words, these are translations of the meanings of names of capital cities
▶ List B contains strange phrases…
▶ ….so make anagrams of these entries. What, for example, is 'Mail' an anagram of?

- ▶ List C contains various entries that contract to acronyms, so take the initial letters
- ▶ For list D, each item is encoded using a cipher provided by the name of the general area to which they all belong
- ▶ Think how the title of 'Salvation Army' could be written in shorthand as a further means of unlocking the theme

25 HAIL!

- ▶ Hail.... who/what?
- ▶ This is an encrypted message, and the person being 'hail'ed hints at the method of encryption
- ▶ You could try breaking the encryption by experimenting with letter values and shifts...
- ▶ ....since this is a Caesar shift

26 VENN 4

- ▶ What do these values remind you of?
- ▶ Something of value perhaps?
- ▶ They are coin values
- ▶ They are common coin values in two specific countries

27 FLAG TIME

- ▶ How can flags be used to communicate letters?
- ▶ And what connection can the time have with the way flags are held?
- ▶ Look up semaphore

28 FIRST REVISIONS

- ▶ There is something very much in common between all the answers
- ▶ In fact, as the title suggests...
- ▶ ....only the first letter is revised
- ▶ You can use this to work out what was going on at 11pm

29 THE LONG AND SHORT OF IT

- ▶ The poem tells you exactly what to do
- ▶ Long words and short words are important
- ▶ Two-syllable versus one-syllable words specifically

▶ Dits and dahs are terms for dots and dashes...

▶ ....in Morse code

(30) SUFFIX TO SAY

▶ You are looking for words that share a common suffix

▶ Or more specifically, a suffix that can go on each of the initial letters given to make the things described

(31) TANGLED TRIOS

▶ The first is to do with Star Trek...

▶ ....and Spock, in particular

▶ While the second is a question of counting it out

▶ Of the remainder, five are triumvirates of characters, and the others refer to a book and to a common phrase

(32) FOUR BY FOUR 3

▶ The first clue is solved as 'HIDE'

▶ And the second as 'WAYS'

▶ In the grid, you need to place a 'C' at top-left

▶ And you need to place a 'S' at bottom-right

(33) NO MAN'S LAND

▶ Is each line roughly the same length? Why might that be?

▶ Do you have the complete alphabet on each line?

▶ What's missing?

(34) MIDDLESIX 3

▶ The top-left letter is a T

▶ And the bottom-right letter is an A

▶ The middle of the grid contains the letter L

(35) ANYTHING ELSE?

▶ It would be a good idea to see what measure is equivalent to 568ml, and how that might match up with the word list

▶ Since it is a PINT, how does that match any of the words – there are two that are close, letters-wise, but you need only one of these

▶ And a sea barrier, spelled the US way, is a groin

- ▶ Each word loses a letter relative to its clue
- ▶ Keep track of the deleted letters to answer the question in the title

36 CRYPTIC MOVIE CLUB I

- ▶ REASON: split it into three words
- ▶ A-LEVEL: it's a word surrounding another
- ▶ PASTA: a word and an abbreviation
- ▶ HECTARE: it's an anagram
- ▶ ADAGES: an abbreviation plus a word
- ▶ WINO: an abbreviation, a word and a letter
- ▶ INSOLE: two words

37 ODD CLUE OUT

- ▶ There is an unusual common property between all but one of the answers
- ▶ The odd-one-out has a very similar property, but in reverse
- ▶ 'The Big Sleep' is of what movie genre?
- ▶ A 'theatrical stand-in' is an understudy

38 MORTPANTEAUX

- ▶ The title is a big clue
- ▶ It is a variation of portmanteaux
- ▶ Although if the title were to be written in the same way as the rest of the clues, it would be just 'ER'
- ▶ Each entry is written using a consistent logic, rather than being an arbitrary combination
- ▶ The length of each 'properly spelled' word is given
- ▶ FOON should be written as SPORK

39 STEP-BY-STEP

- ▶ The 'step-by-step' is very important – you need to continually transform what's left in this puzzle
- ▶ But first of all you need the first step – so can you find a way to read the first line?
- ▶ Using A=1, B=2, etc you need to break the first line up so it makes sense...

▶ ...and you will need to do the same thing for every line from here on

▶ Line 1 gives you an instruction – so do this to all of the following lines

(40) POKER PUZZLE

▶ In the second line, four values out of 10JQQA are correct, as are four out of JQKAA in the third line, and four out of 10JQAA in the fifth line

▶ If 10 was in the hand, we'd need four of the JQKAA values in the third line to match three each from the remaining JQAA and JQQA – so we'd have to have 10JQAA as the overall set of values. But this can't be correct, since it contradicts the first line – so 10 is not in the hand

▶ This means the hand contains JQQA and JQAA, so must be JQQAA, in some order

(41) APT PROPERTY I

▶ Split the word in two equal halves, and see what property each half has, compared to the two halves of a larger set

HINTS FOR CHAPTER 5: ENIGMATIC

(1) ODD PAIR OUT I

▶ The key word here is 'joined' – you will be joining the words into pairs

▶ However, something extra is needed when joining them

▶ An extra letter is needed to join them

▶ But that extra letter differs in some way for one pair

(2) TWO'S COMPANY 2

▶ You are given certain letters from each set of words, with missing letters consistently shown

▶ An underscore means a single missing letter

▶ An asterisk is a wild card for any number of letters, including zero

▶ The first set, and two others, can be counted out

▶ One set gets more specific...

▶ ...and another could be clued synonymously as a 'precipitative knot'

(3) FLOWERS OF THE UK

▶ These are flow-ers

▶ They're UK flow-ers, apart from one

▶ Each word contains a hidden river

(4) GRIDFILL I

▶ The top-left letter is a 'B'

▶ The bottom-right letter is a 'W'

▶ The top-right letter is an 'I'

▶ And the bottom-left letter is a 'T'

(5) PROJECT RUNWAY

- ▶ Use the chart to make deductions, using a tick for a known association and a cross for anything known not to be associated
- ▶ Once you learn that x and y go together, apply any deductions you've already made about x on to y as well
- ▶ Frank was first
- ▶ Greta used runway 25L
- ▶ PUZ-59D was third

(6) TAKE A LETTER

- ▶ The 'logical and consistent way' must be fairly specific to give this puzzle a unique answer
- ▶ You are looking for a way to get from each given word to another that has a very similar meaning
- ▶ You need to remove a letter...
- ▶ ...and then solve the anagram of what's left
- ▶ So, for example, PILFER minus P is an anagram of RIFLE, which has a similar meaning
- ▶ And then you can apply the same rule to the word you obtain from the removed letters, to get the solution letter

(7) WORD MAESTRO

- ▶ What language does 'maestro' originate from?
- ▶ Can you think of English words which have the meanings given?

(8) POP SUMS I

- ▶ Which artists performed 'Smalltown Boy' and 'More Than In Love'?
- ▶ The artists in the example are Bronski Beat and Kate Robbins
- ▶ And what do you notice about those two names?
- ▶ The names are anagrams of one another

(9) RUN THE GAUNTLET

- ▶ In the context of 'run the gauntlet', what is the etymology of 'gauntlet'?

▶ Do these phrases have single-word equivalences in English?

(10) WORD BLUFF

▶ What is the word etymology for 'bluff'?
▶ Can you think of single words that define each of the given entries?

(11) OLD AND NEW

▶ Each word can be replaced with a synonym, or in one case by an abbreviation with the same meaning
▶ Combine the synonyms into pairs that all share the same property. So for example, dawdler and post go together once they have been replaced with their synonyms
▶ Another pair is speechless and movie
▶ Each pair forms a retronym
▶ A retronym is a term for something old that now has to be distinguished from something more recent because it is no longer sufficiently unique. For example, the original version of tennis is now called 'real tennis'

(12) HUNT THE CHARACTER

▶ In the first case for the first component, 'supply... as' functions as an anagram indicator in a cryptic clue – you have to form an anagram of 'free moralist', and the definition is 'a prototype'
▶ In the second case, think of a definite article, plus a word meaning 'peculiarity'
▶ In the third case, look at each of the two words and think of a single common letter that each is missing – and then describe both terms with respect to this
▶ Now find a way to link all three answers to the first component
▶ In the clues for the second component, there is no definition so you have to try to deduce from the wordplay alone how each works

▶ In the first case for the third component, think what the three words might have in common if you remove one letter from each, and what those three letters could form

▶ In the second case, think what word could precede each of the three terms

▶ In the third case, think of two separate synonyms of the key word

▶ Put the four words together and they provide both a clue to the answer as well as an anagram of it

(13) VENN 5

▶ You'll need to map this one out

▶ Specifically, there is a geographical connection within each set

▶ Which half of the world is each country in?

(14) MIXED TRIAD

▶ Each clue is a standard UK cryptic clue, albeit somewhat longer than usual – in each case try to identify where the definition is, remembering that it will be at either the start or the end of the clue

▶ In the first and third case, the definition is at the start; in the second case, it is at the end

▶ In terms of the hint, look at the letters that begin and end each clue and consider what they spell in abbreviated form – this will help you to determine the key relationship between the answers to each of the clues

(15) CODED TRIBUTE

▶ You'll need to use a keyword cipher

▶ You could experiment with letter frequency analysis and test substitutions to start to untangle the code, or you could take a guess at the keyword phrase – which you will have come across elsewhere in the book

(16) ISOLATE 2

▶ The middle of the three stars in the left column must have a wall either above or below it...

- ....although in fact it goes above it
- The first star in the first row has a wall immediately to its right

(17) CRYPTIC MOVIE CLUB 2

- AM: this is a word written backwards
- SCREWABLE: this is one word surrounded by another
- TAN: the first half of a word
- VINOUS: two letters and a word
- KEITH: a word that forms a letter sequence from within part of a title
- EVOLVE: a word that has been stripped of its outer letters
- BIG: a word without an abbreviation that can represent a single word

(18) TITLE FEATURES

- Why don't the years match the movies?
- It's easiest to find the connection if you focus on the shorter titles
- There isn't much that can be done to or with these shorter titles – so how about removing a single letter (although that won't be sufficient for every title)?
- There is something hidden in each title
- Another title is hidden within each given title

(19) GRIDFILL 2

- The first row starts with a 'W'
- And the final row starts with a 'L'
- The last letter of the third row is a 'Y'
- And the first letter of the fourth row is an 'E'

(20) GLOBETROTTING 3

- They all have the same number of characters, so that can't be it
- How can the words be 'globetrotting'?
- Try splitting each word into two halves
- What does each half represent?

(21) EVEN MORE TANGLED TRIOS

▶ The first are three Stooges
▶ The second are needed for good hearing
▶ The third is a sandwich
▶ The fourth should be sized up
▶ The fifth is an elemental band
▶ The sixth will completely get you
▶ The seventh and eighth are from movie titles
▶ The ninth comes in various phases

(22) VENN 6

▶ Think about who would compete in each discipline
▶ Specifically, who might be eligible for each?

(23) TIKTAKA 2

▶ The same shape in each grid has the same path route through it, so start by copying from one grid to the other any shape entrances or exits that are already given. Although for some of the shapes you may not be sure of the orientation of the shape in the other grid, you can still make a note that the path must pass through one of a certain set of points
▶ If a shape is against the edge of the grid in one grid, you know the path can't pass through that edge of it in the other grid so mark in bold borders to show where the path *can't* go
▶ Work back and forth between grids, copying potential path extensions to the other grid to see if it remains plausible, given the requirement to enter and exit each shape exactly once
▶ The path travels from the second to the fourth squares in the first row of the first grid
▶ The path travels from the third to the sixth squares in the penultimate row of the second grid

(24) APT PROPERTY 2

▶ To be an equation, there is probably something numerical involved

- ▶ Try replacing the letters with numbers, using A=1, B=2 etc
- ▶ And split EQUATION into two parts, based on a simple rule, so that each part has the same total value

(25) DIGITALLY ENHANCED JIGSAW

- ▶ The answers are very short – too short to all be regular words, so there must be something else going on
- ▶ You need to rewrite the solutions in a consistent way before entering them into the grid
- ▶ How is the puzzle 'digitally enhanced?'
- ▶ These replacements should sound the same, when each character is pronounced
- ▶ Characters include letters and digits
- ▶ For example, MN8 could be 'emanate'
- ▶ And 'emanate' would solve 'arise'

(26) ODD PAIR OUT 2

- ▶ One pair is absent and receive
- ▶ Another pair is bucks and undoes
- ▶ One more pair is distant and open
- ▶ Can you find an antonym of each word in each pair?
- ▶ More than that, can you find a word that works as a single antonym for each pair?

(27) POP SUMS 2

- ▶ Notice that each sum has four artists on the left and a single artist on the right
- ▶ Once you have substituted each of the song titles, you should have four words on the left and one word on the right of each equation

(28) GRIDFILL 3

- ▶ The top-left letter is 'S'
- ▶ The first line of each shaded area reads 'HC'

(29) ALPHABETIC EXTRACTION

- ▶ There are three cipher keys, each one word long

▶ Decode each line with each key – but only one key will
work for each line
▶ Once you have decoded a line, it will make sense that it
matches its original key

(30) FIND THE ACTRESS

▶ Each clue is solved to give a word of the same length
▶ The words need to be connected in some way
▶ Some of the vocabulary is obscure, but can be inferred
once you understand how the words connect – so solve as
many as you can without spending too long on those you
can't yet be sure of
▶ Each solution word is six letters long
▶ You are building a word ladder

Solutions

Every puzzle has not just
a solution, but also an
explanation — not just *what*
is the answer, but *why* is it
the answer? Indeed, for many
puzzles if you can't work
out what to do, and the hints
haven't helped, then try
reading just the first part of
the solution for an explanation
of what's going on, and then
return and solve the original
puzzle armed with the knowledge
of what to do!

SOLUTIONS FOR CHAPTER I: DECIPHERABLE

(I) FLOWER POWER

Each sentence contains a hidden flower, as follows:

- ▶ Iris: A sparkling diamond for the debona<u>ir is</u> the height of fashion
- ▶ Peony: Skilled jewel-cutters sha<u>pe ony</u>x with tools
- ▶ Lilac: Lapis lazu<u>li lac</u>k the wide range of hues found in other jewels
- ▶ Rose: Eu<u>ros e</u>nable the purchase of German garnets
- ▶ Daisy: A gem-buying agen<u>da is y</u>ielding high profits

(2) MOVIE EDITS

Each entry is an anagram of a well-known movie title.

- ▶ Back to the Future
- ▶ Gone with the Wind
- ▶ Schindler's List
- ▶ Saving Private Ryan
- ▶ Forrest Gump

(3) WORD CONNECTIONS

The words are: FIREARM, ARMBAND, BARMAN, MANKIND and, in the middle, ARMCHAIR and CHAIRMAN.

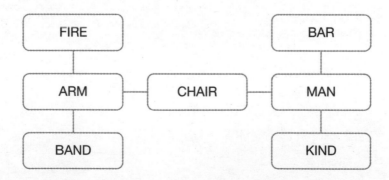

④ END OF SERIES

S: the letters are the final letters in each word of the question, 'What is the final letter in this series?'

⑤ WHAT THE...?

Each listed entry is the name of a Dickens character with its letters reversed, and all of its vowels removed:

- ▶ Llts = Estella
- ▶ Srggj = Jaggers
- ▶ Skrb = Barkis
- ▶ Tswt = Twist
- ▶ Kcwkcp = Pickwick
- ▶ Hctwgm = Magwitch

Therefore the author – Dickens – becomes Snkcd

⑥ CLOCK SCHEDULING

Quarter past seven in the evening. Each word can have 'Battle of' inserted in front of it, and the time then represents the year the battle took place when written using the twenty-four hour clock:

- ▶ 1940 (Battle of Britain)
- ▶ 1815 (Battle of Waterloo)
- ▶ 1945 (Battle of Berlin)
- ▶ 1915 (Battle of Loos)

⑦ COMPLETE THE PICTURE

Each line needs 'ollywood' to be inserted:

- ▶ Dollywood
- ▶ Nollywood
- ▶ Bollywood
- ▶ Hollywood

⑧ PUNAGRAMS I

SPRAIN (pun on sprain and Spain):

- ▶ Belgium (S)

- ▶ Belarus (P)
- ▶ Iceland (R)
- ▶ Slovenia (A)
- ▶ Sweden (I)
- ▶ Serbia (N)

⑨ TETRA-DROP GRID FILL

V	A	C	A	T	E
B	R	I	G	H	T
M	U	F	F	I	N
I	S	L	A	N	D
C	O	F	F	E	E
Z	O	M	B	I	E
S	P	I	D	E	R
C	H	A	R	G	E
B	O	T	T	L	E
S	P	R	I	N	T

⑩ ANAGRAM CONNECTIONS I

The connecting word is CROWD since it can be placed before or after each anagrammed entry to make a new word or term:

- ▶ CONTROL > crowd control
- ▶ OVER > overcrowd
- ▶ FUND > crowd-fund
- ▶ IN > in-crowd
- ▶ PLEASING > crowd-pleasing
- ▶ SOURCE > crowdsource
- ▶ SURFING > crowd-surfing
- ▶ IT > IT crowd
- ▶ MADDING > madding crowd

⑪ TABLE OF RIVERS

Colorado (6), or any other river starting with the letter 'C'. Their initial or first letters conform to the following consecutive elements in the Periodic Table, with their corresponding atomic numbers:

- ▶ Hydrogen (H)
- ▶ Helium (He)
- ▶ Lithium (Li)
- ▶ Beryllium (Be)
- ▶ Boron (B)
- ▶ Carbon (C)

(12) QUOTE HANJIE

Those who can imagine anything, can create the impossible.

(13) PUNAGRAMS 2

HEALIUM: (pun on heal and helium)

- ▶ COPPER (H)
- ▶ ARGON (E)
- ▶ SILICON (A)
- ▶ SODIUM (L)
- ▶ SILVER (I)
- ▶ TIN (U)
- ▶ LEAD (M)

(14) COMMON FEATURES I

They are anagrams of sports:

- ▶ Ice hockey
- ▶ Basketball
- ▶ Triathlon
- ▶ Table tennis

- ► Archery
- ► Badminton

(15) ANAGRAM CONNECTIONS 2

The connecting word is FLOOR since it can be placed before or after each anagrammed entry to make a new word or term:

- ► DANCE > dance floor
- ► SEA > sea floor
- ► BOARD > floorboard
- ► PLAN > floor plan
- ► FIRST > first floor
- ► SHOP > shop floor
- ► TRADING > trading floor
- ► LAMP > floor lamp
- ► PRICE > price floor

(16) ODD NAME OUT I

Hugo: These are all movie titles but only Hugo did not win the Academy Award for Best Picture

(17) COMMON FEATURES 2

They are all words in the English language of Swedish origin

(18) THE VAULT

Echo; Earl; Elan; Envy; Exam; Etch; Ewer; East

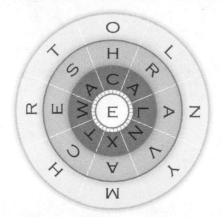

(19) WHERE AM I?

The answers are all US states:

- ▶ Tennessee (ten SE)
- ▶ Illinois (ill in ois)
- ▶ Rhode Island (road island)
- ▶ Montana (M on TANA)
- ▶ New Hampshire (anagram, 'new', of PRIME HASH)
- ▶ Washington (washing ton)
- ▶ Pennsylvania (pencil vein ear)
- ▶ West Virginia (Virginia written 'westwards')
- ▶ Connecticut (connect i to cut)

(20) WATCH THIS

Dalmatians: $(47 - 28) \times 12 - 127 = 101$

(21) COMMON FEATURES 3

They are 'auto-antonyms' in which the same word can have opposite or near opposite meanings:

- ▶ Apology means 'admission of error' or 'formal defence'
- ▶ Back up means 'retreat' or 'give support'
- ▶ Draw the curtains means 'to close the curtains' and 'to open the curtains'
- ▶ Dust means 'to add dust to' or 'to remove dust'
- ▶ Presently means 'immediately' and 'in a while'
- ▶ Sanction means 'permit' or 'restrict'

(22) CAN YOU CONNECT I

They are all things you can 'beat'

(23) ALTERNATIVE EXPRESSIONS I

- ▶ A bird in the hand is worth two in the bush
- ▶ A fate worse than death
- ▶ Famous for fifteen minutes
- ▶ A stitch in time saves nine
- ▶ Cry over spilt milk
- ▶ Fish out of water

(24) ANAGRAM CONNECTIONS 3

The connecting word is LIFE since it can be placed before or after each anagrammed entry to make a new word or term:

- ▶ After > afterlife
- ▶ Jacket > life jacket
- ▶ High > high life
- ▶ Time > lifetime
- ▶ Half > half-life
- ▶ Sized > life-sized
- ▶ Blood > lifeblood
- ▶ Family > family life
- ▶ Cycle > life cycle
- ▶ Guard > lifeguard

(25) SIX MIX I

P	O	R	T	A	L
C	U	R	A	T	E
S	T	R	E	A	M
C	A	M	P	E	D
K	I	N	D	L	E
I	M	P	U	R	E

(26) COMMON FEATURES 4

They are anagrams of titles of William Shakespeare plays:

- ▶ King Lear
- ▶ Pericles
- ▶ The Taming of the Shrew
- ▶ Timon of Athens
- ▶ Romeo and Juliet

(27) KEY NUMBERS

It would represent a call to the emergency services, 911. The code is the notation on a standard English keyboard: !=1, %=5, ^=6, &=7, *=8, (=9,)=0. Therefore:

- Ton=100
- Ice cream with flake=99
- 1815=Waterloo
- 007=fictional spy (James Bond)
- 666=satanic (the devil)

(28) CONNECTION I

They are all meanings of terms that can be prefixed by 'French':

- French press
- French dressing
- French leave
- French toast
- French fries

(29) LITERARY SET

They are all literary titles in which the name of a bird is replaced by its respective collective noun:

- The Crow Road by Iain Banks
- H is for Hawk by Helen Macdonald
- The Owl and the Pussycat by Edward Lear
- The Maltese Falcon by Dashiell Hammett
- The Wings of the Dove by Henry James
- Where Eagles Dare by Alistair MacLean
- Wild Swans by Jung Chang
- Flaubert's Parrot by Julian Barnes
- Shroud for a Nightingale by PD James

(30) MOVIE CLUB I

They are titles of movies in which the name of a US President has been replaced by his successor:

- Charlie Wilson's War
- King Arthur
- The Truman Show
- Get Carter
- Jeremiah Johnson

(31) OBSCENE TITLES

They are titles of movies and books in which a word meaning a shade of blue has been replaced by another:

- ▶ Ocean's Eleven (movie with different versions directed by Lewis Milestone and Steven Soderbergh)
- ▶ Steel Magnolias (movie directed by Herbert Ross)
- ▶ The Royal Tenenbaums (movie directed by Wes Anderson)
- ▶ True Grit (movie with different versions directed by Henry Hathaway and the Coen brothers)
- ▶ Electric Kool-Aid Acid Test (non-fiction book by Tom Wolfe)
- ▶ Alice in Wonderland (children's book by Lewis Carroll)

(32) MOVIE CLUB 2

They are titles of films in which the name of a UK Prime Minister has been replaced by their immediate predecessor:

- ▶ Jackie Brown
- ▶ East of Eden
- ▶ The Blair Witch Project
- ▶ Fifty Shades of Grey
- ▶ Major Dundee
- ▶ North by North West

(33) PUNAGRAMS 3

TWO-LIPS (sounds like tulips)

- ▶ DAHLIA (T)
- ▶ ORCHID (W)
- ▶ GERANIUM (O)
- ▶ VIOLET (L)
- ▶ SAFFRON (I)
- ▶ CLEMATIS (P)
- ▶ LILY (S)

(34) RADICAL TITLES

They are titles of movies, plays, books and songs in which a word meaning a shade of red is replaced by another:

- ▶ Ruby Tuesday (song by The Rolling Stones)
- ▶ Crimson Tide (movie directed by Tony Scott)
- ▶ A Study in Scarlet (book by Arthur Conan Doyle)
- ▶ The Cherry Orchard (play by Anton Chekhov)
- ▶ Brick Lane (book by Monica Ali)

(35) NAVIGRID I

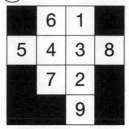

(36) AGENT ACTIVITY

COUNTERINTELLIGENCE:

- ▶ Count
- ▶ Erin
- ▶ (William) Tell
- ▶ I
- ▶ Gen
- ▶ CE (Church of England)

(37) LATELY LONGING

North Pole. It's the places at 0N 0E, 15N 15E, 30N 30E, etc. Although the North Pole is often written as 90N 0E, it could just as well be 90N 90E . The title is a hint to LAT(itude) and LON(gitude).

(38) CONNECTION 2

They define or represent words that begin with three consecutive letters of the alphabet:

- ▶ Defamation
- ▶ Hijab
- ▶ Nope
- ▶ Stucco

▶ Tuvalu

(39) TRAVEL TEST

More – they are anagrams of capital cities:

▶ Copenhagen
▶ Washington, DC
▶ Amsterdam
▶ Rome

(40) FEATURE I

All the words include a silent letter 'l'

(41) SWAP AND SWITCH

▶ CORSET
▶ SOCCER
▶ SCORED
▶ SECOND
▶ COSINE
▶ SOIGNE

The new letters spell CODING

(42) GLOBETROTTING I

▶ A memorial, since the states visited spell MEMORIAL: Maine = ME; Missouri = MO; Rhode Island = RI; Alabama = AL
▶ Cook a meal, since the states spell COOK MEAL: Colorado = CO; Oklahoma = OK; Maine = ME; AL = Alabama
▶ Demand wine, since the states spell DEMAND WINE: Delaware = DE; Massachusetts = MA; North Dakota = ND; Wisconsin = WI; Nebraska = NE
▶ Mainland USA, since the states spell MAINLAND: Massachusetts = MA; Indiana = IN; Louisiana = LA; North Dakota = ND
▶ I therefore avoided saying 'hi', since HI – Hawaii – is the only non-mainland state

(43) FEATURE 2

All the words include a silent letter 'c'

(44) ALPHAHUNT I

The letter P:

```
B A Z T R A U Q H T
P U G K A E I B G C
E W R I N K L E I H
C X M G Y H S K U A
N J E A L O U S Y R
E O D R T A D W F G
L T I E C Y R I Y E
O W U U N I F O R M
I E M A O U S P W V
V F P P O B P E K D
```

Words to find: jealousy; exercise; burglar; wrinkle; uniform; quartz; violence; charge; medium

(45) IN OTHER WORDS

School – it is the lyrics to 'Mary Had A Little Lamb' but in different words. The full nursery rhyme is: 'Mary had a little lamb whose fleece was white as snow. And everywhere that Mary went the lamb was sure to go. He followed her to **school** one day which was against the rules. It made the children laugh and play to see a lamb at school.'

(46) CAN YOU CONNECT 2

They are all things you can set

(47) SPOT THE LINK I

They are words with all of their letters in alphabetical order

(48) SIX MIX 2

T	R	A	V	E	L
D	E	C	R	E	E
R	E	M	O	T	E
D	A	M	P	E	R
C	I	R	C	L	E
A	S	T	U	T	E

(49) SPOT THE LINK 2

They are homographs, i.e. words that can be pronounced in more than one way

(50) CAN YOU CONNECT 3

They are all things you can catch

(51) REBUSES

The connection is that they are all mobile-device applications:

- ▶ Facebook
- ▶ Cut the rope
- ▶ Threes
- ▶ Spotify
- ▶ Dropbox
- ▶ Evernote
- ▶ Instagram

(52) STRIP SEARCH

I was the indefinite article, A. It is describing a sequence where the word is being 'stripped' each time, losing its first and last letters:

- ▶ PIRATES
- ▶ IRATE
- ▶ RAT
- ▶ A

(53) MUSIC MIX

They are all anagrams of songs which were simultaneous number ones in both the UK and the US. Each entry consists of the song title plus the artist:

- ▶ All About That Bass – Meghan Trainor
- ▶ Grenade – Bruno Mars
- ▶ I Kissed a Girl – Katy Perry
- ▶ SexyBack – Justin Timberlake
- ▶ Viva la Vida – Coldplay
- ▶ Shape of You – Ed Sheeran
- ▶ I Will Always Love You – Whitney Houston

(54) SPORTS FILL

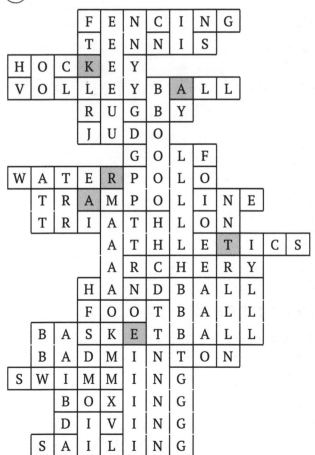

The shaded squares spell out 'KARATE'.

55 GEM OF A PUZZLE

A stone – stones are used in curling; a stone = 14 pounds; to stone is to punish; stones are on the ground; kidney stones are painful; and the title 'gem' hints at a gemstone

56 CAPITAL LETTERS

These clues represent hyphenated words:

▶ B-movie
▶ U-turn
▶ D-Day
▶ A-lister
▶ P-trap
▶ E-layer
▶ S-bahn
▶ T-shirt

The initial letters spell out a capital, BUDAPEST

57 ONE MORE LETTER

▶ Add S to make LEAST
▶ Add T to make STORE
▶ Add R to make GROAT
▶ Add A to make DRAIN
▶ Add V to make VALET
▶ Add I to make PARIS
▶ Add N to make SPINE
▶ Add S to make SPACE
▶ Add K to make STOCK
▶ Add Y to make YEARS

The composer is therefore STRAVINSKY

58 LINK WORDS

▶ BASKET: WASTEBASKET and BASKETBALL
▶ DUST: SAWDUST and DUSTBIN
▶ SPREAD: BEDSPREAD and SPREADSHEET
▶ DRUMS: EARDRUMS and DRUMSTICK

▶ DESCEND: CONDESCEND and DESCENDANT

(59) LATIN PAIRS

V	K	T	L	M	W
M	W	K	T	L	V
W	T	L	K	V	M
K	L	M	V	W	T
L	M	V	W	T	K
T	V	W	M	K	L

1	2	6	5	3	4
3	5	2	4	1	6
5	4	1	3	6	2
4	3	5	6	2	1
6	1	4	2	5	3
2	6	3	1	4	5

K+3=N; M+2=O; L+6=R; V+1=W; W+4=A; T+5=Y, so the solution is NORWAY

(60) DROP ZONE

SOLUTIONS FOR CHAPTER 2: COMPUTABLE

(I) GOING IN BLIND

The secret of this puzzle is to 'go in blind', i.e. to have no eyes, or in other words not to place the 'i's into the grid after you have solved the clues. The solutions to the clues are as follows:

- ▶ DIGIT
- ▶ FIJI
- ▶ FINISH
- ▶ FRIGID
- ▶ HITCH-HIKING
- ▶ IMPLICIT
- ▶ INNING
- ▶ IRIS
- ▶ KIWI
- ▶ LIVID
- ▶ LYRICS
- ▶ MINIM
- ▶ MISSISSIPPI
- ▶ PICNIC
- ▶ PILGRIM
- ▶ SHRIMP
- ▶ SIRI
- ▶ SKIING
- ▶ TIMID
- ▶ TWILIGHT
- ▶ VICTIM
- ▶ VIRGIN

The filled grid looks like this:

(2) PIVOT POINTS

Each word can be mirrored to form a palindrome. The final
letter of the original three-letter word acts as a pivot point:

▶ Madam
▶ Rotor
▶ Tenet
▶ Dewed
▶ Sagas
▶ Level

(3) HOLY ORDERS

They are anagrams of the first five books of the Old
Testament. Solving the anagrams, and then placing the
books in order, gives:

▶ Genesis
▶ Exodus
▶ Leviticus
▶ Numbers
▶ Deuteronomy

Against the original entries, this corresponds to 4, 3, 5, 1, 2

(4) MAN TO MAN

The sequences are as follows:

▶ ROB > MUG > FOOL > JOSH

- ▸ PAT > TAP > BUG > MIDGE
- ▸ NICK > JAIL > CAN > JOHN
- ▸ MARK > SPOT > NOTICE > BILL

⑤ A NEW TERM

Take the first letter of each digit when written as a word, to spell: SENTTEENSOFFTOETON, which can be broken up to read 'Sent teens off to Eton'. In other words, the children were sent to the famous private school, Eton.

⑥ CAN YOU CONNECT 4

They are things you can draw

⑦ ROUTE SUM

The common denominator in the dates of these events is 66, since they are events that occurred in chronological order of centuries from 1066 to 1966 inclusive. The sum of the remaining component in their dates is therefore 145 (10 + 11 + 12 + 13 + 14 + 15 + 16 + 17 + 18 + 19). The title is an oblique reference to the celebrated Route 66, the highway that crosses a large part of the United States.

⑧ NAVIGRID 2

7	6	
	3		1
	8	2	5
	4	9	

⑨ MISFORTUNE

They are the 13th member of noted groups:

- ▸ 13th US President
- ▸ Traditional 13th wedding anniversary symbol
- ▸ 13th book of the Bible (King James Version)

- ▸ The area of the Moon that was the target of the failed Apollo 13 mission in 1970
- ▸ 13th amendment of the US constitution
- ▸ Putative 13th sign of the zodiac

(10) ENDEAVOUR TO SOLVE

The password is ENIGMA. Each sentence of the message contains at least one dot or dash. These correspond to letters in Morse code, with one letter per sentence. Sentence one contains only 'dot', which corresponds to the letter 'E'. Sentence two contains 'dash dot', which corresponds to the letter 'N'. Sentence three contains 'dot dot', which corresponds to 'I'. Sentence four contains 'dash dash dot', which corresponds to 'G'. Sentence five contains 'dash dash', which corresponds to 'M'. Sentence six contains 'dot dash', which corresponds to 'A'.

Here is the letter with the dots and dashes highlighted:

Dear Sarah,

Your letters have been an excellent anti**dot**e to the poor weather in dreary London! I apologize for my own responses being so slap**dash**: I haven't had much time for casual correspondence lately, but don't think me any less **dot**ing than ever! Still, after much a**do t**here's finally been some progress here, and I'm hoping it won't be long before we're ready to sign on the **dot**ted line...

I'm very sorry I had to **dash** Jimmy's hopes about helping with the science project – I'm sure he'll manage just fine without da**da's h**elp though nonetheless, and hopefully you won't be driven too **dot**ty in the process! If you're after something a bit spectacular, a **dash** of vinegar in some baking so**da sh**ouldn't go amiss.

Anyway, I've got to be at Kings Cross at twelve on the **dot**, so I'd better **dash**...

Eternally Yours,

James

(11) ODD NAME OUT 2: VENGEANCE

Scott. These are all first names of Marvel superheroes, but Scott (Lang, Ant-Man) is not an Avenger

(12) ELEPHANT DEVICES

- ▶ The five lines of the treble clef in music: E, G, B, D, F
- ▶ Order of the planets in proximity to the sun (until Pluto was declassified as a planet): Mercury, Venus, Earth, Mars, Jupiter, Saturn, Uranus, Neptune, Pluto
- ▶ Colours of the official five Olympic rings: blue, yellow, red, black and green
- ▶ The first five books of the Bible, known as the Pentateuch: Genesis, Exodus, Leviticus, Numbers, Deuteronomy
- ▶ The five Great Lakes in decreasing size of their surface area: Superior, Huron, Michigan, Erie and Ontario
- ▶ The Mohs scale of mineral hardness on a scale of 1-10: talc, gypsum, calcite, fluorite, apatite, orthoclase, quartz, topaz, corundum, diamond
- ▶ The actors who have played James Bond, in chronological order of appearance in terms of the initial in their surname: Sean Connery, David Niven, George Lazenby, Roger Moore, Timothy Dalton, Pierce Brosnan, Daniel Craig

(13) HIDDEN FLOWERS

There are five rivers ('flowers' – i.e. 'flow-ers') hidden in the text as follows:

- ▶ Po
- ▶ Cam
- ▶ Nile
- ▶ Ouse
- ▶ Tagus

Their positions are highlighted here:

Kew Gardens is a beloved place to sto**p off** to see flowers from across the world. It always provides fantasti**c am**usement to see the exotic names and variety of species.

There have been many new ones placed into the collection, I learn. Even the most zealous enthusiast for flowers would have his or her interest satisfied. One can find useful information everywhere and some people concoct a gushing tribute at the end of their visit.

(14) PISCINE PHRASES

The names of thirteen individual sea creatures are hidden in the statements:

▶ It's supportable a king should abdicate when under pressure
▶ There's no desire in the general population for a long-forgotten church
▶ Toys termed intelligence elements are developed or yet to be used in other rings for spying operations
▶ Tourists escape lines in busy coastal port
▶ The lack of foreign languages in British education is a basic oddity
▶ People stop outside for drinkable treats
▶ All kinds of money emanate easily from a rich aristocrat

(15) FEATURE 3

All the words include a silent letter 'd'

(16) FOUR BY FOUR I

The solution words, and the corresponding filled grid, are as follows:

▶ ASAP
▶ TOPS
▶ REPS
▶ EASE
▶ TRAP
▶ SETT
▶ STAR
▶ TARO

S	T	A	R
E	A	S	E
T	R	A	P
T	O	P	S

(17) TABLE OF COUNTRIES

Sweden (16), or any other country beginning with the letter
'S'. The initial or first two letters in each case conform
to consecutive elements in the Periodic Table, with their
corresponding atomic numbers:

- ▶ Aluminium (Al)
- ▶ Silicon (Si)
- ▶ Phosphorus (P)
- ▶ Sulphur (S)

(18) KLUMP I

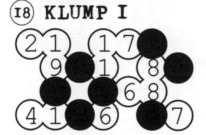

(19) GLOBETROTTING 2

Once represented as international car registrations, the
countries spell out the answers to the questions:

- ▶ MALTA. Countries visited: Morocco (MA), Lithuania (LT),
  Austria (A)
- ▶ PERU. Countries visited: Portugal (P), Spain (E), Burundi
  (RU)
- ▶ IRAQ. Countries visited: Italy (I), Argentina (RA), Qatar
  (Q)
- ▶ I WANT TO TRAVEL FOR AGES. Countries visited: Italy
  (I), Nigeria (WAN), Thailand (T) Tonga (TO), Turkey (TR),

Austria (A), Vatican City (V), Spain (E), Luxembourg (L), Faroes (FO), Argentina (RA), Georgia (GE), Sweden (S)

⑳ VENN I

Left set: letters made from straight lines

Right set: letters made from curved lines

Intersection: letters with both straight and curved lines

㉑ PUNAGRAMS 4

JURASSIC BARK (dog pun on Jurassic Park):

- ▶ SETTER (JU)
- ▶ SAMOYED (RA)
- ▶ GREYHOUND (SS)
- ▶ DALMATIAN (IC)
- ▶ POODLE (BA)
- ▶ BEAGLE (RK)

㉒ ALPHAHUNT 2

The letter D:

```
W Y B O P C F W I H
C U T A U I K Y A M
D Y E T Z B L E U M
E G D O E O U L O A
U M O S I R R I O I
E M S Q G E P J A W
U H N U P A T E X T
F N O I T C A R F I
I D V S P I F K L Y
F W K H S A N G B U
```

Words to find: fraction; viper; squish; aerobic; jerk; pillow; gnash; text; pretty; zoom

(23) ALWAYS ASK WHY

The scores correspond to the number of letter 'y's in the team name, as hinted at by the puzzle title and the final part of the question. So the score was 2 – 1.

(24) WHO'S NEXT?

Taylor, Hurley, or any famous person called Elizabeth. These are the most recent British monarchs from 1820 onwards: George, William, Victoria, Edward, George, Edward, George and then Elizabeth.

(25) FEATURE 4

All the words include a silent letter 't'

(26) WALL TO WALL

The diagonal spells DYNAMO:

¹D	U	V	E	²T	H
E	Y	³H	S	U	R
N	⁴A	N	I	S	⁵E
F	E	⁶R	A	G	L
E	R	E	⁷E	M	B
G	A	T	⁸S	S	O

(27) OBSCURE

A cloud. It's made of water and often returns it as rain. You back up data to a cloud. And as per the title, to obscure is to cloud.

(28) NEXT LINE

APIAPT. The sequence is lines from the song 'The Twelve Days of Christmas', as follows:

- ▶ 5 Gold Rings
- ▶ 4 Calling Birds
- ▶ 3 French Hens
- ▶ 2 Turtle Doves
- ▶ A Partridge In A Pear Tree

(29) WORD FUNKTION

They are meanings of German words for which there are no direct equivalents in English. The title provides a slight clue by translating 'function' into German.

- ▶ Kummerspeck
- ▶ Torschlusspanik
- ▶ Fernweh
- ▶ Wanderlust
- ▶ Schadenfreude

(30) MUDDIED TITLES

They are titles of movies, plays, books and songs in which a word meaning brown, or a shade of brown, is replaced by another:

- ▶ Under Milk Wood (play by Dylan Thomas)
- ▶ Coffee Cantata (secular music composition by Johann Sebastian Bach)
- ▶ Charlie Brown (song by Coldplay)
- ▶ Charlie and the Chocolate Factory (children's book by Roald Dahl)

(31) DOUBLE DUTY NAMES

Bamako. The names of the countries to which four of the cities belong (Greece, Hungary, Denmark, Pakistan) end with a boy's name, while those of four others (Argentina, Rwanda, Canada, Bolivia) end with a girl's name. The name with which the remaining country (Mali) ends is both a boy's and a girl's name.

(32) IT'S ALL AN ACT

Tom Hanks. The central letters spell the names of movies
he has starred in: Toy Story, Big, Saving Private Ryan, Cloud
Atlas:

- ▶ Cuddly toy – toy poodle
- ▶ Fairy story – story teller
- ▶ Think big – big apple
- ▶ Energy saving – saving grace
- ▶ In private – private investigator
- ▶ Meg Ryan – Ryan Gosling
- ▶ Storm cloud – cloud nine
- ▶ Road atlas – Atlas mountains

(33) QUESTION

As suggested by the title, they are all question words. Each
word is missing its first and last letter. The anagrams are
marked with an asterisk:

- ▶ WHO *   (or WHY)
- ▶ WHY   (or WHO *)
- ▶ WHAT
- ▶ WHEN
- ▶ WHERE
- ▶ HOW *

(34) DEPARTURES

Subtract the hour in the time from the minutes ('take your
time') and take the letter at that index from the relevant
destination ('count on the destination') to spell out the
answer: Reykjavik.

Departure	Time		Letter
Brussels	13:15	(2)	R
Melbourne	21:30	(9)	E
New York	06:10	(4)	Y
Kuala Lumpur	04:05	(1)	K
Rio De Janeiro	09:15	(6)	J
Copenhagen	18:25	(7)	A
Antananarivo	19:30	(11)	V
Cairo	17:20	(3)	I
Hong Kong	05:10	(5)	K

35 CAESAR'S FINAL MOVE

The key to solving this puzzle is to apply a 'Caesar' shift to 'move' each letter to its 'final' position. The 'Ides of March' always fell on the fifteenth, which encourages you to try a Caesar shift of fifteen, i.e. to shift each letter through the alphabet by fifteen positions. Once done the name P. E. E. F. McFep becomes E. T. T. U. Brute, or, with the spaces rearranged, 'Et tu Brute'. So he was the murderer.

36 ECOLOGICAL TITLES

They are titles of movies, plays, books and songs in which a word meaning a shade of green is replaced by another:

▶ Parsley Sage Rosemary and Thyme (album by Simon and Garfunkel)
▶ Midnight Express (movie directed by John Schlesinger)
▶ Paris Texas (movie directed by Wim Wenders)
▶ Emerald Tiger (song by Vanessa Mae)
▶ Key Lime Pie (song by Kenny Chesney)

37 NUMERACY

The score is obtained from the Roman numerals ('old numeracy') within the names: ALan scored 50, KeVIn scored 6, CLIVe scored 154, and so TaMMI scored 2,001

(38) EVER-DECREASING CIRCLES

Solve the clue in each circle to give a different value. The path is then 'ever-decreasing' from the start to the lowest value, as shown:

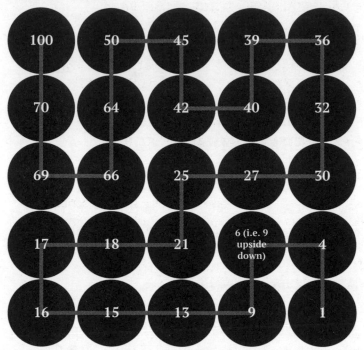

▶ 'Days in four months' refers to the fact that there are four months that all have the same number of days, 30

(39) STEPPING WITH STYLE

As cryptically described in the question, move the first letter one forward in the alphabet, the second two back, and then repeat this for each pair of letters in turn. This results in the question: Which dance means 'double-step' in Spanish? Therefore the answer to the question is 'paso doble'.

(40) TANGLED DUOS

▶ SAPEPPELTR = SALT and PEPPER
▶ SCHONNERY = SONNY and CHER
▶ JUROLIMETEO = ROMEO and JULIET
▶ QUKIENENG = KING and QUEEN

- ▶ BUBTREATEDR = BREAD and BUTTER
- ▶ HARMMODERGESTERINS = RODGERS and HAMMERSTEIN
- ▶ MISKSEPIRGMIGTY = KERMIT and MISS PIGGY
- ▶ GADOBBALNACE = DOLCE and GABBANA
- ▶ BARTOBINMAN = BATMAN and ROBIN
- ▶ EADAVEM = ADAM and EVE
- ▶ CANTLEOHOPANTRAY = ANTHONY and CLEOPATRA
- ▶ BETAHEUBETASTY = BEAUTY and THE BEAST
- ▶ POCALLSTORUX = CASTOR and POLLUX
- ▶ MALUIRIGIO = MARIO and LUIGI
- ▶ PETELNLERN = PENN and TELLER

(4I) HEADS OF STATE

Abraham Lincoln, who was sixteenth – this is describing the US presidents on the face of Mount Rushmore. Lincoln was the sixteenth president.

(42) SAVAGE BRACKETS

The words are grouped (bracketed) into sets of three, and in each case you are looking for a word which can prefix all three in the set to form a new word or phrase. These then form their own sets of three which work in the same way, and then finally these combine again one more time for the leftmost word, WILD – thus creating 'savage brackets'.

		GAME	BOY
			SHOW
			THEORY
	CARD	SHARK	BAIT
			FIN
			TANK
		TABLE	FOOTBALL
			SALT
			MANNERS
		FORCE	FIELD
			OUT
			MAJEUR
WILD	LIFE	INSURANCE	FRAUD
			POLICY
			AGENT
		SCIENCE	FICTION
			PARK
			MUSEUM
		FIELD	MOUSE
			TRIP
			HOCKEY
	RICE	PAPER	TRAIL
			BAG
			CLIP
		CAKE	MIX
			WALK
			TIN

(43) SUPERMARKET SHENANIGANS

50. Each letter is replaced by its position in the alphabet, and then the sum of its constituent letters gives the value of a word. For example, given that A=1, B=2 and so on then BANANA=2+1+14+1+14+1=33

(44) VENN 2

Left set: square numbers

Right set: even numbers

Intersection: even square numbers

(45) A STARTING CODE IS INVOLVED

The puzzle consists of seven hexadecimal numbers, which are encoded in ASCII as hinted at by the title, whose 'starts' (initials) spell ASCII. In ASCII, 57 = W, 65 = e, 6C = l, 63 = c, 6F=o, 6D=m and 65=e, which spells out 'Welcome'.

(46) DEPECHE CODE

The first letter of the tracks spells out 'INDEX ARTIST BY MINUTE'. 'Index by' means to take the letter at a certain position (index), and to do so based on the value of the minute. For example, for 'Isn't She lovely' by Stevie Wonder, the track length is 1 minute (and 38 seconds) so take letter 1 of the artist's name, as indicated by '1 minute'. This results in 'S'.

If you do this for all tracks, you spell out 'SECONDS MINUS FIFTEEN'. This is instructing you to take 15 seconds off the number of seconds in each track, resulting in 23, 8, 5, 14, and so on. Convert these numbers to letters using A=1, B=2 etc, which translates to WHEN STUCK USE A DE-CODA, the answer, which is itself a musical pun on the word DECODER.

(47) FOUR BY FOUR 2

The solution words, and the corresponding filled grid, are as follows:

- ► FIVE
- ► IDEA
- ► ESSE
- ► VEST
- ► LESS
- ► FOLD
- ► ODES
- ► DATE

F	I	V	E
O	D	E	S
L	E	S	S
D	A	T	E

48 BEEPING MAD

Morse code – 'Morse' is literally written in the middle of the **Ti**mor Se**a**

49 SECONDS AND THIRDS

As the title suggests, the sequences are the second and third letters of words:

- ► EN: numbers from oNE to tEN
- ► RI: days of the week from sATurday to fRIday
- ► LU: chemical elements by atomic number from hYDrogen to fLUorine
- ► IO: colours of the rainbow from rED to vIOlet
- ► IN: US presidents from wAShington to lINcoln
- ► IS: signs of the zodiac from aRIes to pISces

50 BACKWORDS

EXCAVATED, for example, or another word meaning 'MINED'. These are definitions of words when reversed:

- ► STRAP -> PARTS
- ► RAW -> WAR
- ► STRESSED -> DESSERTS
- ► DENIM -> MINED

(51) SCRATCH THAT

A key:

- ▶ Something key is essential, and a key is a common term for islands in the Caribbean
- ▶ A key on a map explains it
- ▶ A musical key sets the sound of music, plus you use keys on a piano to make notes
- ▶ To key a car is to scratch it, as in the title of the puzzle

(52) ON DEAF EARS

These are all words with silent letters. The silent letters themselves spell GOLDEN, which is something that 'silence is'.

(53) MIDDLESIX I

	F	D	F	
P	U	R	E	E
S	T	I	N	G
C	O	N	C	H
	N	K	E	

(54) COME AGAIN?

Each clue refers to a word that has the same set of letters repeated twice, of which only the first set is indicated by the underscores and question marks. The question mark letters spell out, appropriately, CAN YOU REPEAT THAT.

▶ French dance	Cancan
▶ Latin American dance	Cha-cha
▶ New York prison	Sing Sing
▶ Good vision and a form of cricket	Twenty twenty
▶ Extinct bird	Dodo
▶ African dish made from semolina	Couscous
▶ Caused by lack of vitamin B1	Beriberi
▶ Bloodsucking African fly	Tsetse
▶ Cheerleading accessory	Pom-pom

- ▶ German spa town   Baden Baden
- ▶ Musical 'Lady'   Gaga
- ▶ 'Millionaire' life-line   Fifty-fifty
- ▶ Plaque   Tartar
- ▶ Hawaiian fish   Mahi mahi
- ▶ Nickname of both the Pope and Hemingway Papa
- ▶ Drum and sat-nav brand   TomTom

55 SO IT BEGINS (AND ENDS)

Each word starts and ends with the same two letters:

- ▶ CHURCH
- ▶ INSULIN
- ▶ HEADACHE
- ▶ EMBLEM
- ▶ ESCAPES
- ▶ MAGMA
- ▶ ETHERNET
- ▶ DECIDE
- ▶ PHOTOGRAPH
- ▶ NECKLINE

56 ALTERNATIVE EXPRESSIONS 2

- ▶ Laughing stock
- ▶ Fair and square
- ▶ Lame duck
- ▶ Rocket science
- ▶ Vicious circle
- ▶ Face the music

57 SPY LOGIC

The solution is:

- ▶ Natalia Zukova – Lipstick camera
- ▶ Valentina Pavlova – Toothbrush flash drive
- ▶ Kristina Karpova – Nail polish transmitter

SOLUTIONS FOR CHAPTER 3: TESTING

(I) UK TRANSPORT PREDICTIONS

The twelve common items are names of UK shipping forecast areas, to which the title is a cryptic reference. They are referred to as follows:

As first parts of noted geographical place names:

▶ Portland Bill (promontory in Dorset)
▶ Trafalgar Square (in central London)
▶ Plymouth Hoe (open public space on the seafront in Plymouth)

As surnames of well-known figures:

▶ Donovan Bailey (Canadian athlete who won the 100 metres gold in the 1996 Olympics)
▶ Carrie Fisher (US actress)
▶ Dick Lundy (US animator who developed Donald Duck)

As homophones:

▶ Sole/Soul
▶ Faeroes/Pharaohs
▶ Wight/White

As anagrams:

▶ Dogger/Gorged
▶ Hebrides/Bed Hires
▶ Fastnet/Fattens

(2) FIVE BY FOUR

The sets are:

▶ Pac-Man ghosts: BLINKY, PINKY, CLYDE and INKY
▶ Apples: FUJI, JAZZ, DISCOVERY and RUSSET
▶ Types of sweet: BOILED, CHEWY, FIZZY and SOUR

- ▶ Shades of brown: TAN, FAWN, CHOCOLATE and CHESTNUT
- ▶ Slang for parts of the body: PINS, HOOTER, MUG and NOODLE

(3) THE MAN WITH THE GOLDEN PUN

Like the title to the puzzle, each motion picture is the name of an actual Bond movie but with one letter changed. The movies are:

- ▶ For your ewes only (For Your Eyes Only)
- ▶ Licence to bill (Licence to Kill)
- ▶ Tomorrow never lies (Tomorrow Never Dies)
- ▶ A view to a hill (A View to a Kill)
- ▶ The world is hot enough (The World is Not Enough)
- ▶ Die another May (Die Another Day)
- ▶ Casino Royals (Casino Royale)
- ▶ Er, no (Dr No)
- ▶ You only jive twice (You Only Live Twice)

(4) NEXT IN LINE I

Each list is a sequence of either initials or letters as follows:

- ▶ U: Mercury Venus Earth Mars Jupiter Saturn **Uranus** (planets in our solar system)
- ▶ S: first second third fourth fifth sixth **seventh**
- ▶ M: I (1) V (5) X (10) L (50) C (100) D (500) **M (1000)** – Roman numerals in increasing value
- ▶ S: March April May June July August **September**
- ▶ T: Friday Saturday Sunday Monday Tuesday Wednesday **Thursday**

(5) ESCAPED ANIMALS

The animals, and the restored sentences, are as follows:

- ▶ Lion: It's the dol<u>l I on</u>ly used to play with my friend
- ▶ Zebra: Which si<u>ze bra</u>s will be most suitable for modelling in the lingerie department?
- ▶ Snake: Hear<u>s nake</u>d woman putting on clothes after bathing

▶ Camel: Male be<u>came l</u>ast to finish the race, having fallen first

▶ Bear: Is a bul<u>b ear</u>ly to rise from their bed in the spring?

(6) DIVERSITY TEST

The sequence consists of the initials of book titles which contain colours by their respective authors, the length of whose names are given. The books are given in the order of the colours of the rainbow: red, orange, yellow, green, blue, indigo and violet. Violet therefore has to be deduced. The title hints at the use of the rainbow as a symbol for diversity.

The book titles are:

▶ The Hunt for Red October by Tom Clancy
▶ A Clockwork Orange by Anthony Burgess
▶ Crome Yellow by Aldous Huxley
▶ Anne of Green Gables by Lucy Maud Montgomery
▶ Porterhouse Blue by Tom Sharpe
▶ Indigo by Alice Hoffman
▶ Any book with 'violet' in the title will work here, such as Shrinking Violet by Lou Kuenzler (3,8)

(7) LIFE FORMS

The transformation from the first to the second column is to find an anagram of the word; then from the second to third column it is to find a homophone of the word. The third column consists solely of animals:

DOTE	TOED	TOAD
ROBE	BORE	BOAR
KILNS	LINKS	LYNX
ASHORE	HOARSE	HORSE
DARE	DEAR	DEER
TEACHER	CHEATER	CHEETAH

⑧ KEY WORDS

They are words that can be spelled exclusively with either the left-hand or the right-hand side of a QWERTY keyboard, respectively

⑨ SEQUENCE I

The next item in the sequence would be Yosemite or any other National Park in California (Death Valley, Golden Gate, Joshua Tree, Kings Canyon, Lassen, Mojave, Pinnacles, San Francisco Maritime, Santa Cruz, Santa Monica, Sequoia). The sequence is of national parks in US states heading west along the Mexican border from Texas to California.

⑩ HOUSE-HUNTING

They are the royal houses of England and Great Britain:

▶ Norman (Wisdom, perhaps; anagram: Roman n)
▶ Angevin (area of western France; anagram: given an)
▶ Plantagenet (Latin sprig of broom; anagram: get plate ann)
▶ Lancaster (bomber; anagram: clear stan)
▶ York (bowl; anagram: ry – ok)
▶ Tudor (architectural style; anagram: tour d)
▶ Stuart (Little, perhaps; anagram: a trust)
▶ Orange (fruit; anagram: on grea)
▶ Hanover (German city; anagram: hear nov)
▶ Windsor (Barbara, maybe; anagram: in words)

This leaves Saxe-Coburg-Gotha as the missing royal house.

⑪ FINAL AGENT

A different word can be added to each set in turn. Together the words spell out LIVE AND LET DIE, the 1973 Bond movie starring Roger Moore

▶ LIVE: alive, olive, outlive, relive
▶ AND: brigand, errand, riband, thousand
▶ LET: goblet, leaflet, pallet, tablet

▶ DIE: baddie, caddie, foodie, indie

(12) WORD ASSOCIATION

A poorly dressed woman. The numbers represent the sequence number of US presidents and the words give definitions of their names with the initial letters switched to the letter given in brackets:

▶ 11 = folk/Polk
▶ 14 = fierce/Pierce
▶ 18 = orant/Grant
▶ 27 = daft/Taft
▶ 29 = warding/Harding
▶ 38 = cord/Ford
▶ 39 = barter/Carter
▶ 41 and 43 = gush/Bush Senior or Junior
▶ 45 = frump/Trump

(13) THEMED PAIRS

The four pairs comprise meanings of words that begin or end with the name of a particular metal. Therefore the pairs must be selected as follows:

▶ Starring/implore = leading/plead
▶ Glittering paper/swift-flying songbird = tinsel/martin
▶ De-creasing/firedog = ironing/andiron
▶ 18th century Irish dramatist/flower with yellow or orange heads = Goldsmith/marigold

(14) MUSICAL WORDS

They are words that consist entirely of letters that represent musical notes – A, B, C, D, E, F, G:

▶ Acceded
▶ Baggage
▶ Cabbage
▶ Defaced
▶ Effaced
▶ Facade
▶ Gagged

(15) A BIT TO EAT

Each of the ticks can be read as a '1' in a binary number, with the absence of a tick representing a '0'. A single binary digit is called a 'bit', thus the title of the puzzle. The puzzle also refers to the values of the form 2^x that are the decimal equivalent of a binary digit: $2^0 = 1$ = 'one', $2^1 = 2$ = 'too', $2^2 = 4$ = 'for', $2^3 = 8$ = 'ate', $2^4 = 16$ = 'six teen'-agers.

The orders are shown converted to decimal in this table:

	Apple pie 16	Ice cream 8	Burger 4	Fries 2	Drink 1	Total value
Anne		✓				8
Barney		✓	✓	✓	✓	15
Coleen	✓		✓			20
David			✓			4
Erica		✓	✓	✓	✓	15
Frank			✓	✓	✓	7

The question refers to the 'A1 Cafe', which is a hint that A=1. Continuing with B=2, C=3 and so on, the values can then be converted into letters: 8=H, 15=O, 20=T, 4=D, 15=O, 7=G.

So the missing item was a HOTDOG.

(16) VENN 3

Left set: Countries

Right set: Five-letter words

Intersection: Five-letter countries

(17) EXTRA

They are definitions of things that are examples of RAS syndrome, or Repetitive Acronym Syndrome syndrome – in other words, acronyms where the last word is often repeated after the acronym itself. The title is intended to suggest the nature of the link:

▶ ATM machine (Automated Teller Machine machine)
▶ LCD display (Liquid Crystal Display display)

▶ SALT talks (Strategic Arms Limitation Talks talks)
▶ HIV virus (Human Immunodeficiency Virus virus)
▶ PIN number (Personal Identification Number number)

(18) IT'S ALL GREEK TO ME

The four groups comprise words in the English language that have Greek prefixes: para, cata, hypo and hyper. The groups are as follows:

Para:

▶ Parachute (one way to leave an aircraft)
▶ Parador (Spanish hotel)
▶ Parapet (wall)

Cata:

▶ Catacomb (underground burial site)
▶ Catatonic (suffering an abnormality of movement and behaviour)
▶ Catastrophe (disaster)

Hypo:

▶ Hypoblast (tissue type)
▶ Hypodermic (type of syringe)
▶ Hypothesis (possible scenario)

Hyper:

▶ Hyperbole (exaggeration)
▶ Hyperlink (computing connection)
▶ Hypermarket (superstore)

(19) AUTHORITATIVE COMMENTS

They are all sayings or excerpts of speeches made by US presidents with the vowels removed, and the spaces rearranged:

▶ Read my lips: no new taxes – slogan used by George H W Bush
▶ The only thing we have to fear is fear itself – broadcast by Franklin D Roosevelt

- My fellow Americans! Ask not what your country can do for you. Ask what you can do for your country – speech by John F Kennedy
- I never trust a man unless I've got his pecker in my pocket – comment by Lyndon B Johnson
- If you want a friend in Washington, get a dog – comment attributed to Harry S Truman
- Blessed are the young for they shall inherit the national debt – Herbert Hoover
- You may fool all the people some of the time; you can even fool some of the people all the time; but you can't fool all of the people all the time – speech by Abraham Lincoln

(20) CLIMBER'S DIVISION

The noted group are members of the Ivy League – hence the 'Climber's Division' title. The members of the group given by each clue in turn are as follows:

- Brown (in Rhode Island) – UK Prime Minister, Gordon Brown
- Columbia (in New York) – homophone ('broadcast') of Colombia, South American country
- Cornell (in New York state) – former US grunge musician, Chris Cornell
- Dartmouth (in New Hampshire) – British naval college
- Pennsylvania (in Pennsylvania) – reference to the Pennsylvania Dutch
- Princeton (in New Jersey) – Prince (singer) + ton (weight)
- Yale (in Connecticut) – key supplier

Harvard (in Massachusetts) is therefore the missing member of the group

(21) PERIODIC PAIRS

The items are prefixes to different days of the week, denoting events in the religious, sporting and social calendar:

- Cyber and Plough for Monday

- ▶ Shrove and Super for Tuesday
- ▶ Ash and Spy for Wednesday
- ▶ Black and Maundy for Thursday
- ▶ Casual and Good for Friday
- ▶ Holy and Lazarus for Saturday
- ▶ Bloody and Palm for Sunday

(22) BACK TO THE BEGINNING?

The numbers correspond to the lengths of US presidential surnames. The only other ten-letter surname of a US president is George WASHINGTON – hence the title 'Back to the Beginning?' So the correct letter to write in is 'W':

- ▶ 4: Bush × 2 (HW + W), Ford, Polk, Taft
- ▶ 5: Adams × 2 (John + Quincy), Grant, Hayes, Nixon, Obama, Trump + Tyler
- ▶ 6: Arthur, Carter, Hoover, Monroe, Pierce, Reagan, Taylor + Truman, Wilson
- ▶ 7: Clinton, Harding, Jackson + Johnson × 2 (Andrew + LBJ), Kennedy, Lincoln, Madison
- ▶ 8: Buchanan, Coolidge, Fillmore, Garfield, Harrison × 2 (Benjamin + William), McKinley, Van Buren
- ▶ 9: Cleveland, Jefferson, Roosevelt × 2 (Theodore + FDR)
- ▶ 10: Eisenhower, Washington

(23) LEADERS OF THE GODS

The translation in question is between the Greek name for the god and their Roman name. As the title of the puzzle ('leaders') indicates, the first letter of the name is the relevant one: the number represents how to get from the first letter of the Greek name to the first letter of the Roman name alphabetically.

Therefore, since the Roman name for Dionysus is Bacchus, and 'B' is two letters before 'D' alphabetically, then Dionysus = -2

(24) BILINGUAL GIBBERISH

They are ways of saying something is unintelligible in a different language, and furthermore each compares with a foreign language to do so:

▶ It looks like Chinese (in Filipino)
▶ It's Arabic for me (in Italian)
▶ It's Volapuk to me (in Esperanto)
▶ It's Chinese (in French)

The equivalent phrase used in English would be 'it's all Greek to me', or perhaps 'double Dutch', as suggested cryptically by the title.

(25) PUNAGRAMS 5

The sports, and their added letters, are as follows:

▶ GOLF (L)
▶ ARCHERY (A)
▶ SOCCER (C)
▶ BASKETBALL (K)
▶ SNOOKER (R)
▶ SUMO (O)
▶ WRESTLING (S)
▶ SQUASH (S)

This spells out 'LACK ROSS', which is a pun on lacrosse and the TV show 'Friends'.

(26) KLUMP 2

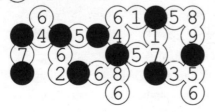

(27) MISSION ACTIVITY

Each word consists of an anagram of a word meaning 'spy', being either a synonym or a real or fictional example of a spy, plus an extra letter. The extra letters left can then be rearranged to form the word ESPIONAGE:

- ▶ PLANT (+i)
- ▶ NARK (+o)
- ▶ MOLE (+n)
- ▶ AGENT (+e)
- ▶ SLEEPER (+s)
- ▶ TOUT (+p)
- ▶ INFORMER (+g)
- ▶ STEED (+a) – John Steed was the suave, bowler-hatted character played by Patrick Macnee in the UK TV series 'The Avengers'
- ▶ BLUNT (+e) – Anthony Blunt was the British art historian and Surveyor of the Queen's Pictures who was publically unveiled in 1979 as a former agent of the Soviet Union

(28) STAGE

They are the names of real-life actors whose first names are also the names of characters in the respective play by Shakespeare:

- ▶ Gertrude Lawrence
- ▶ Rosalind Russell
- ▶ Miranda Richardson
- ▶ Duncan Bell
- ▶ Antonio Banderas
- ▶ Kate Winslet

(29) NUMBER SEQUENCE

The next item in the sequence would be 9 = Rio de Janiero. The sequence is Olympic host cities in chronological order with the sum of the digits in the dates of the Olympic games:

- ▶ Sydney in 2000 = 2 + 0 + 0 + 0 = 2
- ▶ Athens in 2004 = 2 + 0 + 0 + 4 = 6
- ▶ Beijing in 2008 = 2 + 0 + 0 + 8 = 10
- ▶ London in 2012 = 2 + 0 + 1 + 4 = 5
- ▶ Rio de Janeiro in 2016 = 2 + 0 + 1 + 6 = 9

(30) TABLE OF CITIES

Bristol (35 ie Br for Bromine), or any city beginning with 'Br'. The first two letters of each city conform to the following consecutive elements in the Periodic Table with their corresponding atomic numbers:

- ▶ Gallium (Ga)
- ▶ Germanium (Ge)
- ▶ Arsenic (As)
- ▶ Selenium (Se)
- ▶ Bromine (Br)

(31) PERSONAL CONNECTION

They all succeeded their brothers:

- ▶ King John succeeded his brother Richard I (the Lionheart) on the English throne
- ▶ James II succeeded his brother Charles II as the last King of the Stuarts
- ▶ William IV succeeded George IV as the last of the Hanoverians
- ▶ Raúl Castro succeeded his brother Fidel as Cuban President

(32) LANGUAGE TOUR

They are the names of foreign cities in the language of the country indicated in brackets:

- ▶ Mailand (Germany) refers to Milan in Italy
- ▶ Monaco (Italy) refers to Munich in Germany
- ▶ Aix-la-Chapelle (France) refers to Aachen in Germany
- ▶ Rijsel (Holland) refers to Lille in France
- ▶ Wien (Germany) refers to Vienna in Austria
- ▶ Bryste (Wales) refers to Bristol in England
- ▶ Ginebra (Spain) refers to Geneva in Switzerland
- ▶ Pressburg (Germany) refers to Bratislava in Slovakia

(33) BOARD

They are anagrams of types of cheese with an extra letter. The extra letters can then be arranged to form CHUTNEY, a possible accompaniment to cheese. The cheeses are:

- ► Curd (e)
- ► Feta (c)
- ► Brie (t)
- ► Edam (n)
- ► Danbo (u)
- ► Stilton (y)
- ► Pecorino (h)

(34) MIDDLESIX 2

	W	S	B	
P	A	C	E	D
S	T	A	F	F
P	E	R	I	L
	R	E	T	

(35) SEQUENCE 2

The next item in the sequence would be Sunshine. They are the nicknames of the US states along the East Coast, heading in a direction from north to south. The nicknames are as follows:

- ► Ocean (Rhode Island)
- ► Constitution (Connecticut)
- ► Empire (New York)
- ► Garden (New Jersey)
- ► First (Delaware)
- ► Old Line (Maryland)
- ► Old Dominion (Virginia)
- ► Tar Heel (North Carolina)
- ► Palmetto (South Carolina)
- ► Peach (Georgia)
- ► Sunshine (Florida)

(36) ALAN'S CURIOUS QUEST

The clues are chapter titles from the Chronicles of Narnia books. Taking the books in chronological (rather than publication) order, these act as coordinates on the map. For example, 'Lucy Looks into a Wardrobe' is Book 2 Chapter 1, which represents the square in the second column and first row up, as indicated by the '1's at the bottom-left of the grid.

When all the squares with listed chapters are shaded, the word 'Lion.' is spelled out when the page is turned through 90 degrees, as shown below. This answer is also hinted at by the title of the puzzle, 'Alan's Curious Quest' – 'curious' is an anagram indicator, and an anagram of 'Alan's' is 'Aslan', the name of the lion in the Narnia series.

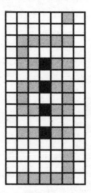

(37) FANDE

They are people who were nicknamed 'The Iron':

▶ The Iron Horse – US baseball player, Lou Gehrig
▶ The Iron Tulip – Dutch football manager, Louis van Gaal
▶ The Iron Duke – British military commander, Arthur Wellesley, 1st Duke of Wellington
▶ The Iron Chancellor – German statesman, Otto von Bismarc

The title refers to 'Fe', the chemical symbol for iron – i.e. 'F and e'.

(38) SEQUENCE 3

They are the opening lines of noted literary works with numbers in their titles in descending order:

- ▶ Seven Pillars of Wisdom by TE Lawrence (autobiographical novel)
- ▶ Six Characters in Search of an Author by Luigi Pirandello (play)
- ▶ Slaughterhouse Five by Kurt Vonnegut (novel)
- ▶ The Sign of the Four by Arthur Conan Doyle (Sherlock Holmes adventure)
- ▶ Three Men in a Boat by Jerome K Jerome (travelogue novel)
- ▶ A Tale of Two Cities by Charles Dickens (novel)
- ▶ One Day in the Life of Ivan Denosovich by Alexander Solzhenitsyn (memoir and novel)

Possible titles to follow could therefore be 'And Then There were None' by Agatha Christie, 'Less Than Zero' by Bret Easton Ellis, or indeed any title that contains either zero or an equivalent word.

(39) EVEN MORE TANGLED DUOS

- ▶ YAYNING = YIN and YANG
- ▶ HALARURDELY = LAUREL and HARDY
- ▶ BIPITESCES = BITS and PIECES
- ▶ SEVERENANUAS = VENUS and SERENA
- ▶ WILKLAIATME = WILLIAM and KATE
- ▶ THEAADILSS = HEADS and TAILS
- ▶ SLANDADERKES = SNAKES and LADDERS
- ▶ PINNEEDLESS = PINS and NEEDLES
- ▶ SCARTIROCKT = CARROT and STICK
- ▶ VECHARPTERSE = CHAPTER and VERSE
- ▶ MOPERSTARTLE = PESTLE and MORTAR
- ▶ FAFUSRIOTUS = FAST and FURIOUS
- ▶ HASMICKMERLE = HAMMER and SICKLE
- ▶ LOPROSFITS = PROFIT and LOSS
- ▶ ALOMPEGAHA = ALPHA and OMEGA

(40) GO WITH THE FLOW

They are the currencies of Asian countries heading in a direct easterly direction. The countries are:

- ▶ Thailand (baht)
- ▶ Cambodia (riel)
- ▶ Vietnam (dong)

The next item in the sequence would be the yuan or renminbi, i.e. Chinese currency

(41) TRANSFORMATION

They are all terms that were devised or coined as a result of anti-German sentiment during World War One:

- ▶ The family name of John Betjeman, the UK Poet Laureate, was originally Betjemann (as they had Germanic roots)
- ▶ The Alsatian was originally called a German shepherd dog
- ▶ The frankfurter was originally renamed 'liberty sausage' until the term 'hot dog' caught the popular imagination
- ▶ Liberty cabbage became the new way of describing the German dish of boiled cabbage, sauerkraut
- ▶ The British royal family changed the name of the royal house from Saxe-Coburg-Gotha to Windsor

(42) TYPES

They are the names of people or places that changed their names for a period of time and then reverted back to their original name:

- ▶ Prince, the pop star, changed his name to an ankh symbol, and then The Artist Formerly Known as Prince, before reverting to Prince in 2000
- ▶ Oslo, the capital of Norway, was called Christiania from 1624 to 1925 before reverting to Oslo
- ▶ Leyton Orient, the association football club located in East London, was renamed Orient before reverting to Leyton Orient

- ▶ Gmail changed its name (in the UK) to Googlemail in 2005 before reverting in 2010 to Gmail
- ▶ Cape Canaveral space centre in Florida was renamed Cape Kennedy in 1963 as a tribute to JFK, before reverting to Cape Canaveral in 1973

(43) MINI BARRED CROSSWORD

Each clue solves to a word that can be phonetically spelled using just letters. For example, 1 across solves to Essex, which can be represented as SX. Therefore you should write 'SX' into the grid in the 1-across position.

¹S	²X	³F	⁴X
A	⁵L	N	S
⁶P	⁷K	⁸D	⁹L
T	¹⁰N	M	E

Across

1. Essex (SX)
3. Effects (FX)
5. Helene (LN)
6. Piquet (PK)
8. Dalziel (DL)
10. Enemy (NME)

Down:

1. Essay (SA)
2. Excel (XL)
3. Effendi (FND)
4. Excess (XS)
6. Peaty (PT)
7. Cayenne (KN)
9. Ellie (LE)

(44) EXCHANGE

They are anagrams of national currencies plus one extra letter. The six extra letters can then be rearranged to form forint, the national currency in Hungary. The currencies are:

- ▶ Rand (+i) – currency of South Africa

- ▶ Leu (+f) – currency of Romania and Moldova
- ▶ Dinar (+n) – currency of Algeria, Bahrain, Iraq and others
- ▶ Lev (+o) – currency of Bulgaria
- ▶ Peso (+r) – currency of Argentina, Mexico and others
- ▶ Euro (+t) – currency of the Eurozone

(45) STATE YOUR NAME

The name pairs contain the hidden names of eleven US cities:

- ▶ ALAN SINGleton (in Michigan)
- ▶ BlaiSE ATTLEe (in Washington State)
- ▶ ConnOR LANDOr (in Florida)
- ▶ DietRICH MONDrian (in Virginia)
- ▶ DoRA LEIGHton (in North Carolina)
- ▶ KlAUS TINdall (in Texas)
- ▶ OgDEN VERnon (in Colorado)
- ▶ PalOMA HArrison (in Nebraska)
- ▶ TrisTAM PArker (in Florida)
- ▶ ViDAL LASsiter (in Texas)
- ▶ ZAK RONson (in Ohio)

The remaining first name Deirdre could for example be paired with a surname beginning NO (e.g. Norton or Norman) to form RENO (in Nevada)

(46) A LAKE IN A COUNTRY?

'Washington' would be an acceptable answer, or any other clue that leads to 'WA'. The title is a cryptic hint to 'Australia' – 'a l' (a lake) in 'Austria' (a country). The group as given consists of the abbreviations of five of Australia's six states, so the remaining entry is WA:

- ▶ NSW (all directions bar East) = New South Wales
- ▶ QLD (question + lethal dosage) = Queensland
- ▶ SA (Salvation Army) = South Australia
- ▶ TAS (teaching assistant + society) = Tasmania
- ▶ VIC (six (VI) + hundred (C), both in Roman numerals) = Victoria

▶ WA (abbreviation for Washington state in the US) = Western Australia

47 ISOLATE I

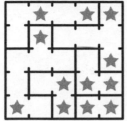

48 TV PUZZLE

▶ 7:00 pm – 2 minutes – art gallery – Martin
▶ 7:15pm – 4 minutes – produce – Pete
▶ 7:30pm – 5 minutes – large cat – Olivia
▶ 7:45pm – 3 minutes – surgery – Nancy

49 TWO'S COMPANY I

The answer is EARTH. Each of the others can join in pairs ('two's company') to form compound words:

▶ RAINBOW
▶ COWBOY
▶ GROUNDHOG
▶ NIGHTMARE
▶ ANYWHERE
▶ BULLDOG
▶ BUTTERCUP
▶ JACKPOT
▶ DRAGONFLY
▶ HORSERADISH
▶ DOWNPOUR
▶ BARCODE

50 FEATURE 5

All the words include a silent letter 'h'

(5I) CONNECTION CLICHÉ

They are meanings of French words and phrases for which there are no direct equivalents in English. The presence of French is obliquely hinted at via the French word 'cliché' in the title. The phrases are:

- ▶ Jolie laide
- ▶ Depaysement
- ▶ Flaneur
- ▶ Trovaille
- ▶ Esprit de l'escalier

(52) FEATURE 6

All the words include a silent letter 'w'

SOLUTIONS FOR CHAPTER 4: ENCRYPTED

I BLETCHLEY PARK CROSSWORD

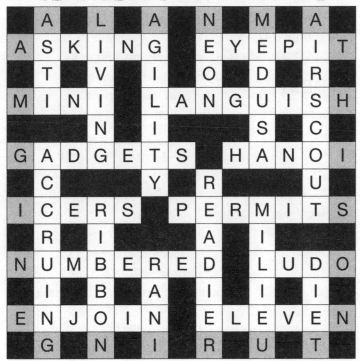

The perimeter letters of the crossword from the top left-hand corner read in a clockwise direction ALAN MATHISON TURING ENIGMA.

Following is an explanation of how the cryptic part of each of the clues works. In 1-down, '& lit.' refers to a clue where the entire clue does double duty as both a cryptic clue *and* definition.

Across

7. ASKING = As king (in a ruling capacity)

8. EYE-PIT = Homophone of 'I Pitt' (personal declaration

by ex-PM, William Pitt)

9.   MINI = MI (military intelligence) + NI (Northern Ireland = province)
10. LANGUISH = L (learner) + anguish (suffering)
11. GADGETS = (Lo)g(ic) + anagram of staged
13. HANOI = H (hotel in NATO phonetic alphabet) + a + no 1 (top)
14. ICERS = (D)icers (people who take risks)
17. PERMITS = IT (modern technology) in perms (waves)
19. NUMBERED = Numb (inactive) + ere (before) + d
21. LUDO = L (lecturer) + u (university) + do (note)
23. ENJOIN = E + n (last letters) + join (connect)
24. ELEVEN = Double definition: eleven=team (side)/ number of letters in the word 'cryptograph'

Down

1.   ASTI = Hidden in (Veron)a's ti(pple) '&lit.' clue
2.   LIVING = Liv(e) (not recorded) + in + G (government)
3.   AGILITY = GI (serviceman) + lit (fired) in a(genc)y (outsiders in agency)
4.   NEON = Hidden in (machi)ne on(ly)
5.   MEDUSA = Med (sea) + USA (home of the CIA)
6.   AIR SCOUT = A1 (capital) + anagram of court's
12. ACCRUING = Homophone of a crewing (a manning of operations)
14. READIER = Die (stop) in rear (back)
16. RIBBON = Double definition; ribbon = fine material in bands/part of typewriter
18. MILIEU = M (spymaster) + I (independent) + lieu (place)
20. RANI = Iran (country) with I at bottom (leader's demoted)
22. DIET = i.e. (that is) in initial letters of decoding team

② COMMON FEATURES 5

They are meanings of homophones of fish:

▶ Place/plaice
▶ Loose/luce
▶ Tuner/tuna
▶ Coddling/codling

③ TIKTAKA I

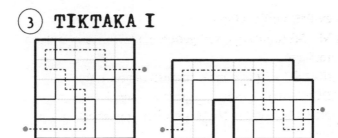

④ WELCOME TO PUZZLANDIA

Each number is of the form x^y – that is, a number raised to a power, as hinted at by the POWER UP message. The first number is 1 to the power of something; the second number is 2 to the power of something; the third number is 3 to the power of something, and so on. This is best discovered by typing some of the numbers into a search engine. Once you have this property, you can type e.g. '7×x' into a calculator and keep pressing '=' until the result on e.g. the seventh line appears, counting the number of presses and then adding 1.

1	=	$1^?$
16,777,216	=	2^{24}
43,046,721	=	3^{16}
1,073,741,824	=	4^{15}
6,103,515,625	=	5^{14}
7,776	=	6^5
678,223,072,849	=	7^{14}
1,152,921,504,606,846,976	=	8^{20}

Since $1^y = 1$ for all values of y, the first exponent could be any number at all. But the remainder are 24, 16, 15, 14, 5, 14, 20 in that order. As the text suggests, you must turn the set of numbers into words. You can do this on the basis that A=1, B=2, etc. Doing this results in ?XPONENT. If you hypothesize an 'E' at the start you end up EXPONENT, which fits the puzzle theme perfectly. This is the answer.

⑤ *** OFF!

Each row has a word to find, with the help of two clues. The clue on the left gives a pun-based description of the answer, and the clue on the right gives a literal description of the answer. The twist, as revealed by the puzzle title, is that you must infer the presence of 'off' after all answers. So a 'Morse contest' is a 'DASH OFF', and also 'Leave quickly' is 'DASH OFF' – but only DASH is indicated by the '? _ _ _' in the table.

Solving each clue ends up with the following:

Morse contest?	**DASH**	Leave quickly
Beauty contest?	**FACE**	Start an ice hockey game
Jazz's Davis's contest?	**MILES**	Nowhere near
Agreement contest?	**NOD**	Go to sleep
Rambling contest?	**WALK**	Get rid of stiffness
Political-slanting contest?	**SPIN**	CSI: Miami or Torchwood
Pedestal contest?	**STAND**	Impasse
Mining contest?	**PICK**	Bring down one by one
Diving contest?	**DROP**	Deliver
Bed-building contest?	**BUNK**	Shirk from work
Timekeeping contest?	**CLOCK**	Stop working
Lumberjacking contest?	**LOG**	Stop working on a computer
Applause contest?	**HAND**	Transfer to another person
Actors' contest?	**CAST**	Remove rope from mooring
Mozzarella-eating contest?	**CHEESE**	Annoy
Theatrical contest?	**SHOW**	Swagger
Election contest?	**VOTE**	Eliminate, as on Survivor
Shouting contest?	**CALL**	Cancel
Relaxing contest?	**LAY**	Fire

Aerial crop-feeding contest?	DUST	Clean after a period without use
CD-making contest?	BURN	Use up energy
Insect contest?	TICK	Complete, as a list
Wrestling contest?	HOLD	Wait

If you read down the letters marked with question marks, which are highlighted in **bold** above, you find that it says DEMOLITION CONTEST LAUNCH.

This is itself another clue in the same vein, to be read like this:

Demolition contest?   _____   Launch

So the final answer is BLAST, since BLAST OFF is 'Launch', and a 'BLAST OFF' could be a 'Demolition contest'.

Although you may not realize you need this extra step at the end just yet, when you get to the final puzzle of this set you will discover you need the word 'BLAST'.

⑥ FEEL LIKE A MEGA HERO

The title is important here – you need to make something that you can 'feel', and in this case it means making Braille characters.

This is a logic puzzle. The numbers in the corner of each rectangle indicate how many circles should be shaded in that rectangle. Meanwhile, the numbers at the end of each row and column show how many circles in that row or column, in the given position, should be shaded.

The puzzle as given has two solutions, unless you realize that a Braille character can't have an empty first row. Using this knowledge, you can work out the unique solution.

Once you have solved the circle-shading part of the puzzle, you obtain:

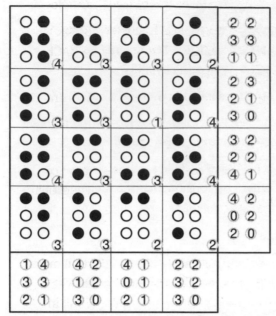

Using an online reference for Braille, you can then read a message as follows: WHO IS MATT MURDOCK?

The answer to the question is: DAREDEVIL, who is a blind superhero, as hinted at by the puzzle title.

⑦ ON THE WAY

The dashes, dots and slashes at the bottom of each box represent Morse code. The slashes show letter breaks, but as given the Morse makes no sense. To read it, you first need to rearrange the pieces into order. The first and last are given, as indicated by the curved sections.

Replacing the pictures with words, you obtain:

COIN	SOCK	HONK	COIL
DIVE	COAL	RICE	HOCK
COAT	FIVE	BOOK	RACK
BOAT	LOCK	HOOK	SACK
BOOT	DICE	RACE	FIRE

These can be rearranged to form a word ladder, as follows:

COIN > COIL > COAL > COAT > BOAT > BOOT > BOOK >
HOOK > HONK > HOCK > LOCK > SOCK > SACK > RACK >
RACE > RICE > DICE > DIVE > FIVE > FIRE

If you now read the Morse code from these tiles in turn, you obtain:

-../ .-./ .-/ ../ -./ ..--../ -/ .-./ .-/ ../ .-..

You can then look up Morse code in a suitable reference. The '..--..' is used for Morse punctuation to indicate a question mark. Converting to text, you obtain:

DRAIN ? TRAIL

Using the theme of the puzzle as a clue, the question mark indicates a missing word. You can read this as DRAIN > ? > TRAIL, and so the missing word is the required link in the word ladder, of TRAIN. This also fits the title, since it is something you might travel in 'On the way'. It's also something you should do for the Puzzlandia championships!

(8) PASSWORD

The words 'poetic scheme' are highlighted, since the puzzle is about poetic schemes. In a poetic (or 'rhyme') scheme, a letter is assigned to each type of rhyme, as follows:

Forgotten the password? (A)

Let me fill you with dread. (B)

I made up this ditty, (C)

So others are deterred, (A)

In a *poetic scheme*. (D)

I'm a literature nerd! (A)

But when parsing it all, (E)

For the line that is third, (A)

Use R instead, (B)

Then go back to C. (C)

What is it you have inferred? (A)

But, the scheme must be modified as described in the poem. Specifically, "For the line that is third, use R instead, Then go back to C." There are two lines with this rhyme, which now becomes R, and the rhymes from D onwards shift one earlier in the alphabet. Applying this logic, you end up with this instead:

Forgotten the password? (A)

Let me fill you with dread. (B)

I made up this ditty, (R)

So others are deterred, (A)

In a *poetic scheme.* (C)

I'm a literature nerd! (A)

But when parsing it all, (D)

For the line that is third, (A)

Use R instead, (B)

Then go back to C. (R)

What is it you have inferred? (A)

The rhyme schemes spell out ABRACADABRA, which is a classical password and the solution to the puzzle.

(9) WHAT'S THE META?

The grid consists of the letters from the answers to the preceding five puzzles: EXPONENT, BLAST, DAREDEVIL, TRAIN and ABRACADABRA. If you trace a path through the grid, from 'ENTER' to 'EXIT', moving between touching squares (including diagonally), and spelling out those words you obtain this:

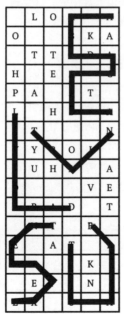

The leftover letters, reading from top to bottom, spell out:
LOOK AT THE PATH YOU HAVE TAKEN. If you indeed do
this, you'll see that you have spelled out five letters:

These spell out, in the order travelled, the overall solution:
SOLVE.

(10) NEXT IN LINE 2

Each list is a sequence of either initials or letters as follows:

▶ S: one two three four five six seven

▶ R: violet indigo blue green yellow orange red

▶ Z: M N B V C X Z (bottom row of a keyboard in reverse order)

▶ N: hydrogen helium lithium beryllium boron carbon nitrogen (elements in increasing atomic number)

▶ F: C G D A E B F# (major keys in increasing order of number of sharps)

(11) KEYWORDS

When using standard predictive text messaging, keying in BARMAID, SMIRNOFF and PINT typically produces CARNAGE, POISONED and SHOT – try it on an old phone!

(12) MIXING PAINT

The words 'rails' and 'fence' hint at using a 'rail fence' cipher, and the repeated reference to 'three' indicates that the cipher should have three rails.

In a rail fence cipher, the plain text is written downwards and diagonally on successive 'rails' of an imaginary fence, then moving up and diagonally when reaching the bottom rail. When the top rail is reached again, the same is then repeated until the entire text is written out. The message is then read in rows, left-to-right and top-to-bottom.

Putting the given text into the 'rail fence' cipher with a key of three gives:

P			L			A			T			W	
	U		P	E		C	R		E	B		O	N
		R			S			L			R		

So the solution is purple, scarlet, brown.

(13) STILL ON THE ROAD

The item in each country is an anagram of the capital city of the country:

- ▶ Serbia > Belgrade > Large bed
- ▶ Algeria > Algiers > Sea girl
- ▶ Australia > Canberra > Care barn

So in Peru you received mail – an anagram of Lima.

(14) MINI 5×5 JIGSAW

Each answer must be written phonetically using letter pronunciations, as follows:

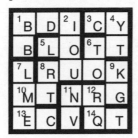

Across:

1.   Intense watch = Beady eye (BDI)
3.   Understand = See why (CY)
5.   Cockney greeting = 'ello (LO)
6.   Monkey = Titi (TT)
8.   Is there a problem? = Are you okay? (RUOK)
10. Void = Empty (MT)
11. Power = Energy (NRG)
13. Here in France = Ici ('here' in French) (EC)
14. Sweetheart = Cutie (QT)

Down:

1.   Netanyahu = Bibi (BB)
2.   You've done me a favour = I owe you (IOU)
4.   Palish = Whitey (YT)
6.   Spanish relative = Tio ('uncle' in Spanish) (TO)
7.   Tropical resin = Elemi (LME)
8.   Bohemian = RT (RT)
9.   Secretive = Cagey (KG)

11. Jealousy = Envy (NV)
12. Disagree = Argue (RQ)

(I5) TWO BOYS

The members of the group are the names given to the beaches in the D-Day landings in Normandy on June 5th 1944. They are Utah, Omaha, Gold, Juno and Sword. Each is referred to in three ways:

▶ Homophonically – 'Echo' group: yew tar, Omagh haar, goaled, Juneau, sord
▶ As a breakdown of their components – 'Breakdown' group: ut (archaic word for 'as')+a+h, OM+a+ha, go+ld, Jun+o, s+word
▶ As associative hints – 'Type' group: another US state, another city in Nebraska, another precious metal, another Roman goddess, another weapon

The title hints to the components of Normandy as Norm + Andy (two boys).

(I6) GC&CS KEYWORD CYPHER

This puzzle requires use of a keyword cipher. In terms of British intelligence, GC&CS refers to the 'Government Code and Cypher School' (note the alternate spelling of 'cipher').

When expressed as a keyword cipher, this becomes a letter-to-letter conversion that looks like this:

G O V E R N M T C D A Y P H S L B F I J K Q U W X Z

A B C D E F G H I J K L M N O P Q R S T U V W X Y Z

The text given in the question can now be decoded to say:

▶ In terms of intelligence, if BENEDICT CUMBERBATCH was ALAN TURING in THE IMITATION GAME depicting events at BLETCHLEY PARK...

...which clues back to the cipher keyword of the 'Government Code and Cypher School', which was housed at Bletchley Park and worked, most famously, on the Enigma machine. Later, it was renamed to GCHQ.

(17) WAVE DOWN

Each country should be converted to its flag, as hinted at by the title and 'flag up'. Each line should be interpreted as an equation with mathematical signs ('sign'), such as a multiplication sign ('cross') or addition operator. Also, 'ripest mix-up' is an anagram indicator for 'stripes', to indicate that you should count the number of stripes to find a number. Therefore the aim of the puzzle is to interpret the flags as mathematical equations.

With this conversion, the clues read:

▶ $3 \times 2 = 6$
▶ $5 + 3 = 8$
▶ $13 \times 0 = 0$

So the final line reads $3 + 3$, and the answer therefore is 6.

(18) OPERATIONS

The thirteen items are code names for Western military operations during the Second War. They are as follows:

1. Michaelmas (US amphibious operation in New Guinea, 1944) – anagram of AIM with MALES around CH
2. Avalanche (Allied invasion of Italy, 1943) – A N CH (Switzerland) in A VALE
3. Overlord (Battle of Normandy in the D-Day landings, 1944) – OVER + LORD
4. Corkscrew (Allied invasion of Pantelleria, 1943) – CORK'S CREW
5. Mincemeat (British disinformation strategy, 1943) – anagram of NICE TEAM ('cooked') after M
6. Cactus (Battle of Guadalcanal, 1942) – CT in CA US
7. Ringbolt (US seizure of Solomon Islands, 1942) – anagram of TROUBLING - U (not 'for all to see')
8. Buffalo (Allied breakout from Anzio, 1944) – double definition
9. Reservist (Allied operation to seize Oran in Algeria, 1942) – double definition
10. Teardrop (US operation to sink U-boats off the eastern

US coast, 1945) – DROP after anagram of TEAR

11. Lumberjack (US operation to capture the west bank of the Rhine, 1945) – LUMBER plus JACK

12. Grenade (Allied operation to cross the Roer river, 1945) – anagram of GRANDEE

The final one to be deduced, in the highlighted column, is Market Garden (Allied airborne and ground operation to encircle the Ruhr, 1944), further hinted at by the initial letters of clues in order: (A) BRIDGE TOO FAR, the title of the book and movie by Cornelius Ryan dealing with the operation.

M	I	C	H	A	E	L	M	A	S	
		A	V	A	L	A	N	C	H	E
			O	V	E	R	L	O	R	D
			C	O	R	K	S	C	R	E	W
		M	I	N	C	E	M	E	A	T
			C	A	C	T	U	S
			R	I	N	G	B	O	L	T
		B	U	F	F	A	L	O
		R	E	S	E	R	V	I	S	T
		T	E	A	R	D	R	O	P
		L	U	M	B	E	R	J	A	C	K
			G	R	E	N	A	D	E

(19) STACKED TIPS

The clues define words in increasing order of length that contain the same three letters at the beginning of the word as they do at the end. As mentioned in the question, each clue gives a full definition of the answer (e.g. 'Expert' = SOPRANO in the first clue), and a cryptic part of only the non-repeated part ('soprano' = S in the first clue):

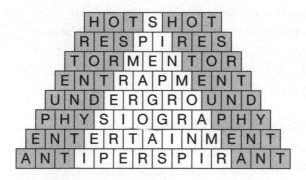

⑳ WORD SQUARE

The answers to the three questions are:

- ► LAN can be inserted into each word to form another word: coLANder, pLANet, seaLANt, sLANting
- ► The real word NIT is a reversal of TIN – all the other words are reversals of meanings of tin: CAN, METAL, MONEY, PLATE
- ► GRU forms the first three letters: GRUb (food), GRUff (rough), GRUnge (US rock music), GRUmble (complaint)

Putting LAN, NIT and GRU into the grid gives:

L	A	N
N	I	T
G	R	U

The name ALAN TURING can then be read by moving horizontally and vertically from letter to letter:

㉑ FIESTA OF FUN

They are meanings of Spanish words for which there are no direct equivalents in English, as hinted obliquely at by the Spanish word 'fiesta':

▶ Sobremesa
▶ Consuegro
▶ Tuerto
▶ Duende
▶ Merendar

㉒ TRANSFORMATIONS

The table at the top defines transformations on the original word, each of which results in an English word:

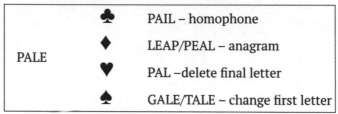

PALE	♣	PAIL – homophone
	♦	LEAP/PEAL – anagram
	♥	PAL –delete final letter
	♠	GALE/TALE – change first letter

These can then be read as instructions to transform each word:

DAMP ♥ DAM ♠ YAM ♦ MAY ♠ LAY ♣ LEI

EARTH ♦ HEART ♥ HEAR ♠ GEAR ♦ RAGE ♥ RAG

STUDY ♦ DUSTY ♥ DUST ♠ BUST ♥ BUS ♦ SUB

STAGE ♦ GATES ♥ GATE ♣ GAIT ♠ WAIT ♣ WEIGHT

YEARLY ♠ PEARLY ♥ PEARL ♥ PEAR ♣ PAIR ♠ HAIR

Which can then be paired with the clues, as required:

▶ Hawaiian garment = LEI
▶ Head covering = HAIR
▶ Heaviness = WEIGHT
▶ Sandwich = SUB
▶ Scrap of cloth = RAG

㉓ NUMBER TRICK

▶ The resulting number, 3,419,670,528, consists of the same ten digits in a different order

▶ The resulting number, 8,549,176,320, again consists of the same ten digits – this time in alphabetical order!

(24) SALVATION ARMY RANKS

The theme is South American countries ('Salvation Army').

List A consists of explanations, or suggested explanations, of their capital cities' names, in terms of the meaning of the underlying native words:

▶ Asunción
▶ Bogotá
▶ Quito
▶ Buenos Aires
▶ Santiago
▶ Montevideo
▶ Lima
▶ La Paz

List B consists of anagrams of the capitals:

▶ Asunción
▶ Lima
▶ Montevideo
▶ Santiago
▶ La Paz
▶ Quito
▶ Buenos Aires
▶ Bogotá

The initials of the entries in list C correspond to their International Vehicle Registration codes:

▶ Rear Admiral = RA = Argentina
▶ Best of luck = BOL = Bolivia
▶ Easily completed = EC = Ecuador
▶ Caught off-guard = CO = Colombia
▶ Physical education = PE = Peru
▶ Pretty youth = PY = Paraguay
▶ Residential care home = RCH = Chile
▶ Ultimately yours = UY = Uruguay

List D consists of their country names enciphered using the cipher South America SOUTHAMERICBDFGJKLNPQVWXYZ, where S should be replaced with A, O with B and so on:

▶ SLMHFPRFS (Argentina)
▶ OGBRVRS (Bolivia)
▶ UERBH (Chile)
▶ UGBGDORS (Colombia)
▶ HUQSTGL (Ecuador)
▶ JHLQ (Peru)
▶ JSLSMQSY (Paraguay)
▶ QLQMQSY (Uruguay)

Each group of four therefore consists of the four items from each country, one from each list.

㉕ HAIL!

The title hints at 'Hail Caesar', indicating the presence of a Caesar shift. Experimentation will reveal that the message has been encoded with a Caesar shift of 16, so to undo the encoding you shift each letter 16 places back in the alphabet, so Q becomes A, R becomes B and so on, to get:

WHICH CAESAR RULED IN THE YEAR (AD) EQUAL TO THE SHIFT USED IN THIS MESSAGE?

The answer to the question is therefore TIBERIUS, since he was the Caesar who ruled in 16AD.

㉖ VENN 4

Left set: Common US coin denominations

Right set: Common UK coin denominations

Intersection: Common coins in denominations used in both the US and the UK

▶ Note that a 50 cent coin was used until relatively recently in the US, but is no longer in general circulation. Other coin denominations have been used historically, but are not in current usage

(27) FLAG TIME

If the times are interpreted as hands on an analogue clock, and then read as semaphore ('flag time'), then the times would spell out TRICOLOUR – the type of flag asked for in the question.

(28) FIRST REVISIONS

Answer: I was having clothes on (or eroding, or anything else that equates to WEARING). With the indexed letter of the alphabet (1am = 0100 hours = A, 2am = 0200 hours = B, ..., 1pm = 1300hrs = M, etc), plus 'earing', I was:

- ▶ 2am: BEARING
- ▶ 6am: FEARING
- ▶ 7am: GEARING
- ▶ 8am: HEARING
- ▶ 2pm: NEARING
- ▶ 6pm: REARING
- ▶ 7pm: SEARING
- ▶ 8pm: TEARING
- ▶ 11pm: WEARING

(29) THE LONG AND SHORT OF IT

If you take a one-syllable word as a dot (or 'dit') and a two-syllable word as a dash (or 'dah'), then each line spells a letter in Morse code: '-.. / .- / ... / .... / .. / -. / --.' This equates to DASHING – which is how Morse could be both 'running' and 'handsome'.

(30) SUFFIX TO SAY

Put letters on the front of ENDER, to make LENDER, SENDER, GENDER, FENDER BENDER. Ender's Game is a book written by Orson Scott Card.

(31) TANGLED TRIOS

- ▶ PROLONGSPLIVERE = LIVE, LONG and PROSPER
- ▶ THRONETWEEO = ONE, TWO and THREE
- ▶ LOBSTARRECLOCKK = LOCK, STOCK and BARREL
- ▶ HARDTRICKYOM = TOM, DICK and HARRY
- ▶ WARWILDROTICOBHEN = LION, WITCH and WARDROBE
- ▶ CARDPAROVERMINAROGOATTSI = PAVAROTTI, DOMINGO and CARRERAS
- ▶ APARTOARHOTMISSHOS = ATHOS, PORTHOS and ARAMIS
- ▶ SCRAPNOCKPLEAP = SNAP, CRACKLE and POP
- ▶ BRAMAROURBRINICEY = BARRY, ROBIN and MAURICE

(32) FOUR BY FOUR 3

The solution words, and the corresponding filled grid, are as follows:

- ▶ HIDE
- ▶ WAYS
- ▶ RIGA
- ▶ CHOW
- ▶ OGLE
- ▶ BEES
- ▶ IDLY
- ▶ CRIB

C	R	I	B
H	I	D	E
O	G	L	E
W	A	Y	S

(33) NO MAN'S LAND

These are sets of letters of the alphabet with letters removed, and the letters removed are then anagrammed to reveal:

- ▶ MEXICO
- ▶ HONDURAS

- ▶ DENMARK
- ▶ UZBEKISTAN
- ▶ SWITZERLAND
- ▶ HUNGARY
- ▶ FRANCE
- ▶ SLOVENIA
- ▶ VIETNAM
- ▶ BELARUS

(34) MIDDLESIX 3

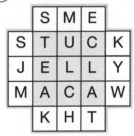

(35) ANYTHING ELSE?

Each clue points to one of the words but with an extra letter. For example, '568ml' represents PINT, compared to the original PIT – so the extra letter there is N. Taken in the order that the words were given, the extra letters spell out ONE MORE THING – answering 'anything else?' in the title.

The words are:

GROIN (sea barrier in the US)   SPARE (extra)

PINT (568ml)   CARTED (carried)

SEVERE (harsh)   HEAT (increase in temp.)

LIMP (walk with difficulty)   PAINT (decorate a wall)

COURT (woo)   PRINCE (monarch's son)

TREE (large wooden plant)   GROUND (soil)

(36) CRYPTIC MOVIE CLUB I

The movies are:

- ▶ About A Boy – re (about) + a son (boy)
- ▶ All About Eve – 'all' around (about) 'Eve'

▶ Dad's Army – pa's (dad's) + T.A. (Territorial Army = army)
  ▶ Bad Teacher – anagram (bad) of 'teacher'
  ▶ Modern Times – AD (Anno Domini = modern) + ages (times)
  ▶ Women In Love – W (women) in 0 (love in tennis)
  ▶ Home Alone – in (home) + sole (alone)

(37) ODD CLUE OUT

The clues result in:

▶ Film noir
▶ Public defender
▶ Gymnopédies
▶ Fed Cup
▶ Understudy

All of the entries contain four consecutive letters, but in 'Fed Cup' they are in descending order whereas in the rest they are in ascending order – so 'Women's tennis team competition' is the odd one out.

(38) MORTPANTEAUX

These are portmanteaux that are the other way around to normal, as indicated by the title. Each word is constructed from the letters not used by the correct portmanteaux:

▶ PARIONETTE: MUPPET
▶ ROLETUME: COSPLAY
▶ HOMBAY: BOLLYWOOD
▶ FOON: SPORK
▶ POMERINE: TANGELO
▶ LEAKFAST: BRUNCH
▶ FOKE: SMOG
▶ CAMFORD: OXBRIDGE
▶ EGANTIC: GINORMOUS
▶ BIDEO: VLOG

(39) STEP-BY-STEP

The first line, if you use A=1, ... Z=26, decodes to DIVIDE NEXT LINES BY THREE, once you have split the numbers up as follows:

▶ 4 9 22 9 4 5 14 5 24 20 12 9 14 5 19 2 25 20 8 18 5 5

Applying the instruction to the next line in particular obtains:

▶ 18 5 22 5 18 19 5 14 5 24 20 12 9 14 5 19

If you then apply A=1, ... Z=26 again then the second line reads REVERSE NEXT LINES. Dividing the third line by three gives:

▶ 41502 11312 541921 242541 81191513

If this is then reversed you obtain:

▶ 3 1 5 19 1 18 14 5 24 2 12 9 14 5 2 1 3 11 20 5 14

...which translates to CAESAR NEXT LINE BACK TEN, indicating that we should apply a Caesar shift to the final line.

So if you take the last line and divide by three:

▶ 3913528162252321145132 391 251734211 51814

...and reverse it:

▶ 4 18 15 11 24 3 7 15 2 19 3
  23 15 4 11 23 25 2 26 18 25 3 19 3
▶ DRO KXCGOB SC WODKWYBZRYCSC

...and then Caesar-shift it as described to reveal THE ANSWER IS METAMORPHOSIS

(40) POKER PUZZLE

They hold the following hand:

(41) APT PROPERTY I

All of the letters in the left half (AMBIDE) are from the left-hand side of the alphabet (first thirteen letters), and all of those in the right half (XTROUS) are from the right-hand side of the alphabet (last thirteen letters).

SOLUTIONS FOR CHAPTER 5: ENIGMATIC

(1) ODD PAIR OUT I

The odd pair out is antic and clone. The words can be paired in such a way that the insertion of a letter in the middle of each pair creates a new word. Of these letters, Y is the only one of these letters that is not a (true) vowel:

- ▶ THEREABOUTS
- ▶ ADULTERATED
- ▶ DETERIORATE
- ▶ TRAMPOLINES
- ▶ PASTEURISER
- ▶ ANTICYCLONE

(2) TWO'S COMPANY 2

Each list is a sequence of words where some letters are missing as follows:

'*' indicates zero or more letters are missing

'_' indicates exactly one letter is missing

- ▶ _EV*: oNE tWO tHRee fOUr fIVe sIX sEVen
- ▶ *ET: rED oranGE yellOW greEN blUE indiGO violET
- ▶ SE*: WHole HAlf THird QUarter FIfth SIxth SEventh
- ▶ SP*: KIngdom PHylum CLass ORder FAmily GEnus SPecies
- ▶ S*H: FirsT SeconD ThirD FourtH FiftH SixtII SeventH

(3) FLOWERS OF THE UK

Vervain. Each of the other words contains a UK river (or 'flow-er'): Fal, Cam, Ure, Usk, Ouse. Conversely, Vervain contains a French river: Ain

(4) GRIDFILL I

B	L	U	I
N	G	E	N
A	R	E	D
I	O	G	I
V	L	L	O
T	E	Y	W

(5) PROJECT RUNWAY

- ▶ 1st – Frank – 25R – PUZ-7CL
- ▶ 2nd – Greta – 25L – PUZ-4E2
- ▶ 3rd – Dana – 36L – PUZ-59D
- ▶ 4th – Eli – 36R – PUZ-9N3

(6) TAKE A LETTER

In each case a single letter can be removed, and the remaining letters then rearranged, to make a second word of a similar meaning.

- ▶ PILFER - P = RIFLE
- ▶ BLABBER - R = BABBLE
- ▶ NOMINATE - A = MENTION
- ▶ ENQUIRED - N = QUERIED
- ▶ CLATTER - C = RATTLE
- ▶ TRIFLE - E = FLIRT
- ▶ BASTE - S = BEAT

This spells out 'PRANCES', from which the letter 'N' can be removed to make the word 'CAPERS', which just like in all of the cases above has a similar meaning to the original word. So the solution is 'N'.

(7) WORD MAESTRO

They are meanings of Italian words, as obliquely hinted at by the word 'maestro' in the title, for which there are no direct single-word equivalents in English:

▶ Abbiocco

▶ Gattara

▶ Meriggiare

▶ Ciofeca

⑧ POP SUMS I

The names of the artists most commonly associated with each song form anagrammatic equations, so the example can be converted as follows:

▶ Smalltown Boy *becomes* Bronski Beat = More Than In Love *becomes* Kate Robbins

...since 'Bronski Beat' is an anagram of 'Kate Robbins'.

All songs in this question were top 20 hit singles in the UK, but can also be looked up in an online search engine to find their original artists.

Using the same logic to rewrite the first question in the puzzle:

▶ One Week *becomes* Barenaked Ladies = Make It With You *becomes* Bread + _____

...so you are looking for a recording artist whose name, when combined with the letters in 'Bread', is an anagram of 'Barenaked Ladies', or in other words is an anagram of 'NAKELADIES'. Such an artist is Neil Sedaka, so you can pick any Neil Sedaka song to complete the first equation. So the following is a valid solution, for example:

▶ One Week = Make It With You + Laughter in the Rain

The second equation can also be rewritten similarly:

▶ Viva La Vida *becomes* Coldplay + Big Log *becomes* Robert Plant + The First Picture Of You *becomes* Lotus Eaters = Pure Morning *becomes* Placebo + Refugees *becomes* Tears + _____ + _____

...so you are looking for two recording artists, whose names, once combined, form an anagram of 'COLDPLAYROBERTPLANTLOTUSEATERS' minus

'PLACEBOTEARS', or in other words two artists which together form an anagram of 'DLYORPLNTLOTUATERS'.

As can perhaps be seen from the starting letters of the anagram, the artist Dolly Parton can be extracted, leaving 'LTUTERS', which is itself an anagram of the artist Turtles. So to complete the equation, you need two songs – one by Dolly Parton, and one by Turtles. So a valid solution is:

▶ Viva La Vida + Big Log + The First Picture Of You =
  Pure Morning + Refugees + Jolene + Happy Together

⑨ RUN THE GAUNTLET

'Gauntlet', as used in the phrase 'Run the gauntlet', is a word of Swedish origin. These are meanings of Swedish words for which there are no direct equivalents in English:

▶ Mysa
▶ Fika
▶ Harkla
▶ Lagom

⑩ WORD BLUFF

They are meanings of Dutch words for which there are no direct equivalents in English. If you look up 'bluff' in a dictionary you will see it is of Dutch origin. The Dutch words are:

▶ Uitbuiken
▶ Uitzieken
▶ Uitwaaien
▶ Afbellen
▶ Gedogen
▶ Gezellig

⑪ OLD AND NEW

The terms have to be paired to form a series of retronyms – these are neologisms for things that have been superseded or supplemented by other more modern versions of the item. Each term, when replaced by a synonym, can be combined with another to form such a neologism:

- ▶ Presumptuous + cut = forward slash (neologism created after the advent of the backslash)
- ▶ Dawdler + post = snail mail (neologism for regular post created after the advent of electronic mail)
- ▶ Speechless + movie = silent film (neologism for an early film without speech, after the advent of the talkie)
- ▶ Actual + racket sport = real tennis (neologism for traditional tennis created after the advent of lawn tennis)
- ▶ Standard + cooker = conventional oven (neologism created after the advent of the microwave oven)
- ▶ Unbending + match = straight marriage (neologism created after the advent of same-sex marriages)
- ▶ Morning + transmit = AM radio (neologism created after the advent of FM radio)
- ▶ Broadsheet + reserve = paper book (neologism created after the advent of e-books)
- ▶ Aural + axe = acoustic guitar (neologism created after the advent of the electric guitar)

12 HUNT THE CHARACTER

The three hints for the first component are solved as follows:

- ▶ Supply free moralist as a prototype (8, 4) clues EARLIEST FORM ('free moralist' supplied as – anagrammed as – a word meaning 'prototype')
- ▶ AN is an 'article', and 'peculiarity' can mean 'oddity' – so the answer is 'AN ODDITY'
- ▶ 'pe' and 'imittion' are both words meaning 'to copy' that are missing an 'a' ('ape' and 'imitation'), or in other words can be described whimsically as 'NOT A COPY'

EARLIEST FORM, AN ODDITY and NOT A COPY are all clues to the answer AN ORIGINAL.

The cryptic clues making up the second component are solved like this:

- ▶ 'Drink covering good cups?' clues ALGEBRA: ale (drink) around g (good) + bra (cups?)

▶ 'Record freeze falling short' clues LOGIC: log (record) + ic(e) (freeze falling short)

▶ 'Hardened skin around much of incision' clues CALCULUS: callus (hardened skin) around cu(t) (much of incision)

ALGEBRA, LOGIC and CALCULUS are examples of MATHS.

The third component is solved as follows:

▶ Demon, taupe and notion are anagrams of words meaning 'head', plus an extra letter: dome + n, pate + u, onion + t, which spells out 'nut' – another word for 'head'

▶ Case, hatch and shell can be preceded by 'nut' to make new terms

▶ Polish and cool clue 'buff' and 'fan', which are synonyms for 'nut' as e.g. in the phrase 'I'm a sports nut/buff/fan'

Overall you now have AN ORIGINAL MATHS NUT, which is both a clue to and an anagram of ALAN MATHISON TURING.

(13) VENN 5

Left set: Countries in the northern hemisphere

Right set: Countries in the southern hemisphere

Intersection: Countries that are in both the northern and southern hemispheres

(14) MIXED TRIAD

They are the respective meanings of TERGIVERSATION, REINVESTIGATOR and INTERROGATIVES, which are considered to be the longest non-scientific words in the English language that are anagrams of each other. The initial and last letters of each clue in order spell out AN ANAG, which is an additional hint.

▶ T (Thailand) + ER (monarch) + GIVER (donator) + [O (round figure) in SATIN (material with sheen)]. Definition = 'Altering sides'

- ▶ REIN (A strap) + VEST (clothing) + [ROTA (schedule) + GI (serviceman)] (reversed). Definition = 'person who studies matter again'
- ▶ [E (English) + R (Republican)] in ('engaged in') INTRO (start) + [GATES (billionaire) around IV (four)]. Definition = 'As an example, who and why'

(15) CODED TRIBUTE

This puzzle requires use of a keyword cipher. This is based on Alan Turing, using his full name of ALAN MATHISON TURING. When expressed as a keyword cipher, this becomes a letter-to-letter conversion that looks like this:

A L N M T H I S O U R G B C D E F J K P Q V W X Y Z

A B C D E F G H I J K L M N O P Q R S T U V W X Y Z

The text given in the question can now be decoded to say:

Recognized as a FOUNDING FATHER of ARTIFICIAL INTELLIGENCE with creations such as the AUTOMATIC COMPUTING ENGINE among his works, this pioneer created the TURING MACHINE which became a landmark in its field.

His final research was entitled THE CHEMICAL BASIS OF MORPHOGENESIS (published in 1952) describing the way in which non-uniformity may arise naturally out of a homogeneous, uniform state.

(16) ISOLATE 2

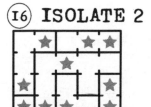

(17) CRYPTIC MOVIE CLUB 2

- ▶ The Mummy Returns: ma (mummy), reversed (returns)
- ▶ Men In Black: crew (men) in sable (black)

- ▶ Half A Sixpence: tan = half of tanner (sixpence)
- ▶ The Sixth Sense: VI (the sixth) + nous (sense)
- ▶ Some Like It Hot: hidden (some) in 'liKE IT Hot'
- ▶ The Naked Gun: revolver (gun) without its 'clothing' (naked)
- ▶ A Life Less Ordinary: biog (a life (story)) less O (Ordinary)

(18) TITLE FEATURES

They contain the titles of other noted movies:

- ▶ If (1968 movie directed by Lindsay Anderson)
- ▶ Heat (1995 movie directed by Michael Mann)
- ▶ Ray (2004 movie directed by Taylor Hackford)
- ▶ Ran (1985 movie directed by Akira Kurosawa)
- ▶ Z (1969 movie directed by Costa-Gavras)
- ▶ Babe (1995 movie directed by Chris Noonan)
- ▶ Argo (2012 movie directed by Ben Affleck)

(19) GRIDFILL 2

	W	E	N
P	R	A	V
C	I	T	Y
E	D	H	N
G	T	T	O
L	U	S	L

The words with the same meaning are WEN and CITY.

(20) GLOBETROTTING 3

The words represent journeys between pairs of the world's hundred busiest airports:

- ▶ MAD-DEN = MADRID-DENVER
- ▶ SEA-MAN = SEATTLE-MANCHESTER
- ▶ BOM-BOS = MUMBAI-BOSTON
- ▶ LAX-IST = LOS ANGELES-ISTANBUL

▶ HEL-LAS = HELSINKI-LAS VEGAS

Of these, BOM-BOS is the longest journey, at 12,239 km (7,605 miles), so is the 'longest' word.

(21) EVEN MORE TANGLED TRIOS

▶ CLAMOURRELYRY = LARRY, MOE and CURLY
▶ SHAMTIMERRRANUVIPL = HAMMER, ANVIL and STIRRUP
▶ BLEATTCOMATOUTCONE = BACON, LETTUCE and TOMATO
▶ LSMEARMADIGULLME = SMALL, MEDIUM and LARGE
▶ FEARWITHINRED = EARTH, WIND and FIRE
▶ SHINLIKEROOKNE = HOOK, LINE and SINKER
▶ BAGDOUGLODY = GOOD, BAD and UGLY
▶ PALTUTORAMAINEOBINSLESS = PLANES, TRAINS and AUTOMOBILES
▶ SLOGAILSQUIDID = SOLID, LIQUID and GAS

(22) VENN 6

Left set = Olympic athletic events competed in by men

Right set = Olympic athletic events competed in by women

Intersection = Olympic athletic events competed in by both men and women

(23) TIKTAKA 2

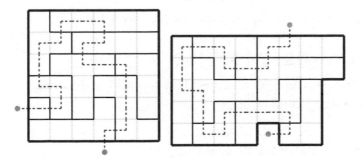

24 APT PROPERTY 2

The sum of the alphabetical values of its vowels (5 + 21 + 1 + 9 + 15), and that of its consonants (17 + 20 + 14), both equal 51 – thus forming a beautiful EQUATION!

25 DIGITALLY ENHANCED JIGSAW

Each answer must be written phonetically using letter and digit pronunciations, as follows:

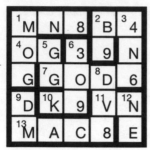

Across:

1. Arise = Emanate (MN8)
2. Earlier = Before (B4)
4. S-shaped moulding = Ogee (OG)
7. Shortest lines between points = Geodesics (GOD6)
10. Dog = Canine (K9)
11. French river and department = Vienne (VN)
13. Waste away = Emaciate (MAC8)

Down

1. Pictogram = Emoji (MOG)
2. Not harmful = Benign (B9)
3. Scientific crime department = Forensics (4N6)
5. Horse = Gee-gee (GG)
6. An essential amino acid = Threonine (3O9)
8. Stray = Deviate (DV8)
9. What's seized in Latin = Diem (DM)
12. Whichever = Any (NE)

26 ODD PAIR OUT 2

The odd words out are darkness and heavy. All the words form pairs which share an antonym (opposite), but all of the other pairs are also heteronyms (same spelling, but different pronunciations and meanings):

▶ Present (absent/receive)
▶ Sow (boar/reap)
▶ Does (bucks/undoes)
▶ Supply (demand/rigidly)
▶ Close (distant/open)

By contrast, the two meanings of light, as antonyms of darkness and heavy, are not heteronyms – both have the same pronunciation.

(27) POP SUMS 2

First notice that each left-hand side contains four artists, and each right-hand side contains only one artist. The theme here is four-word song titles that are themselves made up of four successive one-word song titles. Each artist on the left is therefore to be replaced by an appropriate one-word song that they are associated with, and when these words are combined it will create a song associated with the artist on the right.

In the example:

▶ Elvis Presley (Don't) + Coldplay (Talk) + Radiohead (Just) + Prince (Kiss) = Right Said Fred (Don't Talk Just Kiss)

The equations can then be solved like this:

▶ Spice Girls (Goodbye) + Olivia Newton-John (Sam) + Adele (Hello) + Kenny Ball & His Jazzmen (Samantha) = Cliff Richard (Goodbye Sam Hello Samantha)
▶ Ashford & Simpson (Solid) + Spandau Ballet (Gold) + Commodores (Easy) + Sweet (Action) = T. Rex (Solid Gold Easy Action)

All the songs were top 20 hit singles in the UK.

(28) GRIDFILL 3

S	E	O	H	C
A	L	B	I	A	S
H	C	U	L	O	S
T	A	S	D	N	A
T	I	P	E	R	I

(29) ALPHABETIC EXTRACTION

There are three keys: 'car', 'house' and 'factory' which can be used to decode the letters on each key. Each key should be 'inserted' into the alphabet, as also suggested by the title, 'alphabetic extraction'.

You can then use the modified alphabet to extract text from each numbered key. For example, using the 'car' key you can read each numbered key as follows:

C	A	R	B	D	E	F	G	H	I	J	K	L
A	B	C	D	E	F	G	H	I	J	K	L	M

M	N	O	P	Q	S	T	U	V	W	X	Y	Z
N	O	P	Q	R	S	T	U	V	W	X	Y	Z

This decodes to Key 1 = VLOHQDLM, Key 2 = AUTOMOBILE and Key 3 = QFRESFLUF. Of these, only Key 2 = AUTOMOBILE makes sense, and also matches up with this being the 'car' key – so key 2 is the car key.

Using similar logic you can use the 'factory' key to deduce that 1 = WORKSHOP, thus identifying key 1 as the factory key, and you can use the 'house' key to deduce that 3 = RESIDENCE, meaning that key 3 is the house key.

(30) FIND THE ACTRESS

Each phrase is a clue to a six-letter word:

- ▶ Angled   FISHED
- ▶ Baby's shoe   BOOTEE

▶ Body louse	COOTIE
▶ Curbed	BITTED
▶ Mountainside basin (Scot)	CORRIE
▶ Punched	FISTED
▶ Scrounged (Aust)	BOTTED
▶ Soccer	FOOTIE
▶ Started up (a computer)	BOOTED
▶ To potter	FOOTLE
▶ To snuggle (Scot)	COORIE
▶ Town near Liverpool	BOOTLE
▶ Was of the correct size	FITTED

Once you have a few of the answers, you might spot that they are very similar, and further that you can build a word ladder:

CORRIE > COORIE > COOTIE > FOOTIE > FOOTLE > BOOTLE > BOOTEE > BOOTED > BOTTED > BITTED > FITTED > FISTED > FISHED

At this point you can now 'find the actress' – if you add an extra word to both the start and end of the word ladder you can now change CARRIE to FISHER in 14 steps.

So the solution is Carrie Fisher.

Authors

The puzzles in this book were
edited by Gareth Moore, who also
wrote the hints and the solution
explanations.

The following puzzle authors created all of the puzzles for this book:

ANTHONY PLUMB

Anthony Plumb is a school teacher, living in Lincolnshire, England. He has enjoyed puzzles all his life, and especially crosswords. He writes them for various UK publications, including The Telegraph, The Financial Times and The Independent newspapers.

DANIEL PEAKE

Daniel Peake is a quiz and puzzle constructor from Reading, England. Writing quizzes from the age of 10, he has worked on BBC shows including Beat the Brain, Two Tribes and Only Connect. He also recently constructed murder mystery cases for television. He specializes in wordplay-based puzzles.

DAVID MILLAR

David Millar is an American puzzle author with more than a decade of puzzle-writing under his belt, and whose puzzles have previously featured in both UK and World Puzzle Championships. He lives in Fort Worth, Texas.

GARETH MOORE

Gareth Moore is the author of over 75 books of puzzles for both children and adults, and the creator of the daily brain-training site, BrainedUp.com. He creates all types of puzzle, ranging from crosswords and other word puzzles through to sudoku and logic puzzles, and all the way on to complex dot-to-dot, colour-by-number and maze books. He also creates sticker books and other types of activity content, as well as optical illusions, quizzes and trivia books.

He has written several books of brain and memory training puzzles, exercises and tips, and frequently appears on TV and radio as both a brain-training and a puzzle expert. His puzzles also appear in apps, on websites, in magazines and in newspapers, as well as in board games. He is also a board member of both the World Puzzle Federation and the UK Puzzle Association.

GUY CAMPBELL

Guy Campbell is a writer and designer from London. Responsible for over 30 books, including The Boy's Book of Survival, he also writes puzzles for newspapers and magazines in the UK, Australia, India, Scandinavia and France. He is also a keen poker player, and writes quiz questions for both TV shows and for Trivial Pursuit.

LAURENCE MAY

Laurence May is a software developer and backgammon enthusiast who has been inventing logic puzzles since he became obsessed with sudoku in 2005. Laurence's creations are regularly published in the UK in both the Times and Daily Mail newspapers, and have been featured in puzzle magazines around the world. He lives in Buckinghamshire, England, with his wife, two teenage daughters and a tiny cockapoo.

MICK HODGKIN

Mick Hodgkin is a journalist and cryptic crossword compiler, writing under the handles of Morph and Micawber. As Mick Twister (@twitmericks), he writes news limericks on Twitter and is the author of There Was an Old Geezer Called Caesar: A History of the World in Limericks (Anova, 2013) and There Once Was a Man With Six Wives: A Right Royal History in Limericks (Pavilion, 2017).

MIKE TURNER

Mike Turner writes quiz questions and puzzles across all types of media. He is Senior Writer for the BBC Two lateral thinking show Only Connect, specializing in writing the connecting walls. He has also written questions for BBC quizzes The Code and Decimate. He also researches obscure facts for the BBC Radio 4 programme The Museum of

Curiosity, writes a weekly puzzle for the Radio Times and has provided content for various quizzing and puzzle apps.

In front of the camera, Mike has won many TV quiz shows in the UK, including 15 to 1 and The Weakest Link Champions League.

PHILIP MARLOW

Philip Marlow has worked in television journalism and social research. He compiles cryptic and general knowledge crosswords for several national UK newspapers, including The Telegraph, Financial Times and The Independent, where his guises are Shamus, Sleuth and Hypnos. He sets questions for BBC TV quiz shows, including Only Connect and University Challenge.

RICHARD HEALD

Richard Heald is a mathematics graduate and IT worker who lives in South Yorkshire, England. He has been a long-time fan, and occasional setter, of puzzles and quizzes, and was a series semi-finalist on the UK TV quiz shows Only Connect and Countdown. He has a particular love of competitive crossword solving and has on several occasions been the annual champion of The Observer newspaper's Azed clue-writing competition (see www.andlit.org.uk). He also served for five years as clue judge for The Crossword Club.

ZOE WALKER

Zoe Walker is a professional puzzle editor, and has worked on a number of puzzle books. She holds an M.Phil in Philosophy from the University of Cambridge, which may explain her fondness for puzzles which require deep thinking.